Where Witchcraft Lives

Doreen Valiente

4th Edition

Design & Layout: Ashley Mortimer / The Doreen Valiente Foundation
Cover Artwork: Tony McLeod © 2010

Printed by Lightning Source International

Published by The Doreen Valiente Foundation
in association with The Centre For Pagan Studies

First published 1962
Second Edition 2010
Third Edition 2011
Fourth Edition 2014

ISBN   978-0-9928430-1-4

www.doreenvaliente.org
www.centre-for-pagan-studies.com

The Witch at Hallowe'en

She passes through the village street
As twilight shadows fall.
The full moon climbs the winter sky,
The trees are bare and tall.
What is the secret that they share,
Shadow and moon and tree,
And little laughing breeze that makes
The dead leaves dance with
glee? They know their kin.
The owl cries His greeting out to her.
Now the last house and garden's past,
The Down's ridge rises bare.
A climbing moonlit path she sees
That was a trodden road
Ere conquering Rome or Norman proud
O'er Downland ever strode.
It leads to where, beneath the turf,
The outlines she can trace
Of barrow and of sacred ring
That mark the old gods' place.
The moon rides high. The years roll back,
Are with her garments shed.
Naked she dances out the ring
First wrought by hands long dead.
The blood leaps wild within her veins
As swifter spins the dance,
Her wide eyes fixed upon the moon,
Her senses rapt in trance,
And though no feet of flesh and blood
Walked with her to that ground,
She knows she does not dance alone
That magic circle's round.

Introduction

When reading Doreen's books it is apparent that she is weaving her research and poems into the fabric of her spirituality, authenticating the facts for herself, so that she could impart this knowledge on to others. This is truly her magical legacy.

When I started my quest for knowledge about Witchcraft over 40 years ago, there were very few books written on the subject. Most of those that I found were either inaccurate or defamatory. When I first picked up Where Witchcraft Lives I was not living anywhere near Sussex, and having read the first couple of chapters I realised that the book was more about the research of an area rather than Sussex itself. For me the book was a revelation. I truly could identify with the author though it had me wondering why this person calling herself a student was able to have so much access to this hidden society we call the Craft.

By coincidence my musical career saw me living in Sussex many years later and wanting to consult the book again as I was on the spot, I discovered that it was no longer in print. It was while living in Sussex that I met my wife Julie. A few years later Julie and I along with a couple of well respected friends set up the Centre for Pagan Studies. One night Doreen Valiente turned up at one of our events. I can remember being very nervous when she wanted to meet me, but we became instant friends. We soon discovered Doreen had a wicked sense of humour. Keen on what we were doing at the CFPS, she later asked us if she could get more involved and despite her protestations that she was not worthy enough, she became our patron and I became her final working partner and high priest. Doreen's last ever public appearance entitled "An Afternoon with Doreen Valiente" and was for the Centre For Pagan Studies.

It is worth noting that Doreen referred to herself as a "student" in this book even though at this point she was already initiated. The reason she gave to me when I asked her about this was that she did this out of respect for her aging mother who was still alive at this time and a very strict Christian; she did not want to offend her or have her mother face ridicule at the church where she attended.

Unfortunately in 1999, Doreen became very ill and soon after died of cancer. She asked me to arrange and preside over her funeral. She also bequeathed to me her famous collection of artefacts, saying that I would know what to do with it when the time came. Before she died, she said that it was her wish to have her poems as a stand alone book, so posthumously we published many of them in the 'Charge of the Goddess' on her behalf. This was so named after her well-known poem of the same name.

I have no doubt in my mind that Doreen Valiente's contribution to the understanding of the "Craft of the Wise" is immeasurable. For me she is by far the most important figure we have seen to date. Her place in history is secure and when you study the Craft in detail, you will understand why Doreen's name appears in the Oxford Dictionary of National Biography.

Over the years we have had hundreds of emails asking about this book as it was no longer in print. In this limited edition version we have added photographs; some are from the Doreen's own collection of artefacts and others provided by her beloved Brighton Museum and Sussex Archaeological Society, without whose original research and later support Doreen's exploration would have been considerably harder.

All the proceeds of this book will go towards the costs of setting up the Doreen Valiente Foundation that will take care of her legacy for all time. A museum and study centre based upon her life's work and that fabulous treasure trove she left behind to be owned by all of us and for all of us who come to the Craft seeking knowledge.

So having met, crafted with and loved one of the nicest and most important people in our all our lives, and someone whom Julie and I are proud to have called a friend, I do hope that you enjoy once more this little piece of history by the most famous of 'student witches'.

Many blessings,

John and Julie Belham-Payne

The Doreen Valiente Foundation and The Centre for Pagan Studies wish to thank: Richard Mark Le Saux, Kate Richardson, Sussex Archaeological Society, Ronald Hutton, Morgana, Alex Gunningham, Tony McLeod and Wapa the cat!

Where Witchcraft Lives

Contents

𝕱oreword

By Ronald Hutton, Professor of History, Bristol University, UK

𝕱or the past half-century, *Where Witchcraft Lives* has featured among the most neglected of texts concerning modern Pagan witchcraft. It has not been classed among those which revealed great traditions of that witchcraft to the wider world, such as the books by or associated with Gerald Gardner, Alex Sanders (as ghosted by June Johns), Robert Cochrane (as represented by Justine Glass), Stewart and Janet Farrar, Ray Buckland or Starhawk. Nor is it among those which have challenged orthodoxies within the movement, such as the works of Aidan Kelly. This is despite the fact that it is very early – indeed one of the first three books to be published on the subject – and the work of the greatest single female figure in the modern British history of witchcraft.

There are two apparent reasons for this relative obscurity. One is that it presented itself as a study of witchcraft in a single county: that of Sussex to which Doreen had just moved, with which she rapidly fell in love, and whichbecameherhomefortherestofherlife. Asaresultitwouldhave seemed to possess less general relevance than others, and her efforts to make her favourite county seem special might have had the effect of making it seem less characteristic of Britain in general. The other is that she had not yet 'come out' as a witch herself, because of the pain that such a public stance would have inflicted upon her family. She therefore assumed the tone of a curious outsider and observer, depriving her writing of the emotional force that was embodied in the works of practitioners who spoke with personal feeling and commitment of their experiences.

None the less, the book has real importance, and deserves to be treated as a classic, for three different reasons. The most obvious is simply that it was the first major published work of such an outstanding figure in Pagan history, and already displays the features which were to be characteristic of her writing and speaking in the rest of her long life: her vivid and lucid style of expression, her openness of mind, her adventurous interest in different traditions and generosity towards their practitioners, and her tremendous talent for composing ritual, especially in verse. The poem published in the introduction is typical of her work, and represents yet another gem in the treasury of emotive and beautiful rhythmic recitation which is probably her most important single contribution to the history of modern religion.

The book also displays another abiding characteristic of hers, of a different kind: her unusual credulity in believing press reports. She assembled a large collection of these, which has survived to become an important resource for an historian, and she depended rather heavily on them for some of her wider impressions of contemporary magic in Britain, with the occasional addition of gossip heard from individuals whom she met. As a result, she felt able to declare in the book that the existence of a sinister and dangerous 'black' magic among the modern British could be denied only by the ignorant and the guilty: a belief which, though apparently based on no first-hand experience, might have been expected to have a significant impact on readers.

Other prominent witches of the period displayed a much more sceptical public attitude towards such rumours and newspaper claims. The truth of the matter remains undecided, making Doreen's approach to it the more interesting and sustainable.

The second remarkable feature of the book is that it remains, until this date, the only one produced by a prominent modern witch that embodies actual original research into the records of the trials of people accused of the crime of witchcraft during the early modern period. Modern witches have customarily identified themselves strongly with the victims of those trials, but have tended to take their impressions of them filtered through the works of historians of varying degrees of reliability. Doreen made the breakthrough of looking at the actual records (at least in publication), and therefore was in a position to be able to write genuine history herself, of a kind the more valuable for being the work of a modern practitioner of the craft concerned.

Unhappily, from this point of view, she placed two limitations on herself. One was that she diffidently interpreted the facts that she was revealing within the framework supplied by the foremost contemporary academic expert in the early modern trials, Margaret Murray. This declared confidently that the people persecuted as witches in these trials had actually been devotees of a surviving ancient pagan religion, dedicated to the fertilising powers of nature. It has subsequently been proved wrong, and by dutifully following it Doreen lost a unique opportunity to evaluate what she was uncovering in its own terms and relate it to modern witchcraft in a new and more accurate way.

The other limitation was that she never again showed an interest in such primary research, preferring ever after to quote from existing works of history, and (as said) no prominent witches have followed her in looking at original records. Her single excursion is therefore the more interesting and valuable.

The final important feature of the book consists of the descriptions of rites carried out by pagan witches at various locations in East Sussex at or just before the time when she was writing. They are notable for their originality and beauty, and Doreen's lyrical descriptions do them full justice. The identity of the people concerned has never been revealed, and so this is apparently a lost part of our history, to which the book is our only witness. One aspect of them alone has passed into wider modern witch tradition, through Doreen: the closing toast,

'To the Old Ones! Merry meet, merry part' (to which is now commonly added 'and merry meet again').

It seems an appropriate point at which to end this brief set of suggestions, in the poignant knowledge that Doreen herself is now one of the greatest of the Old Ones whom we hail in parting.

- Professor Ronald Hutton

A Word from The Author

One beautiful summer's day my husband and I went out into the Sussex countryside, to a place called Rocky Clump, near Stanmer.

This place, a cluster of trees on a hill, is the site of a former pagan temple. Local archaeologists discovered there a number of burials, and a huge stone which they think may have been an altar-stone.

We spent a summer afternoon there, seated among the trees. The nearest other human beings were men working in the fields down in the valley, some distance away. Yet several times, close at hand and seemingly out of the air, we both heard strange chords of music, rather like that of a harp.

We were unable to find any material explanation for it. The date was the anniversary of one of the festivals of the pagan Old Religion, Midsummer Day, June 24th.

After the coming of Christianity, the pagan traditions were banned by the Church. They were driven underground and called witchcraft.

Sussex, of course, is by no means the only county in which they still live on. Witchcraft survives all over Western Europe, and was taken by emigrants to the colonies of America and Australia. However, I have chosen in this book to write mainly of Sussex. This is partly because I wish to write of things I know personally, and partly because Sussex could be taken as a sample of the way in which the strange tapestry of witchcraft has been woven through the centuries.

Before the Roman Conquest, much of Sussex was covered by forest, which stretched from the borders of Kent to Hampshire. The Ancient Britons called this forest Coid Andred. The Romans knew it as Silva Anderida. The Saxons called it Andredsweald or Andreds-lea. Part of the New Forest is still called "Andret" in the Domesday Book.

Some writers have thought this name originally meant "The Black Forest". Others again have taken it to mean '"The Forest Where Nobody Dwells". Still others, however, believe it was so called because it was sacred to an ancient goddess called Andred. It has been suggested that the Big-on-Little rock near West Hoathly, which resembles a gigantic human head, was venerated as a resemblance of this goddess.

According to R. Thurston Hopkins, a well-known Sussex antiquary, the wood in which this rock stands was still known locally up to recent times as Andred's Wood, and shunned after dark as being uncanny. If this is correct, it supports the theory of the goddess Andred, who may well have continued to be secretly worshipped long after Sussex was nominally Christian.

With the coming of the Saxons, the great forest became the refuge for the dispossessed Romano-Britons, and for outlaws generally. Many ancient traditions will have lived on in its wooded glades, to form the older threads in the pattern of Sussex witch-lore.

Aboriginal beliefs will have mingled with such Roman Mysteries as those of Priapus and the Bona Dea. These deities will have been far closer to the ordinary people of those days than such far-off, aristocratic gods as Jupiter or Apollo. Hence their rites, concerned with fertility, the life-force of the land and of men and beasts, will have lived on when Jupiter was but a name.

The Saxons, too, brought with them their own fertility cult, that of the phallic god Frey and his sister Freyja, the goddess of love and magic. They had a lively belief in magic. Each letter of their Runic alphabet was also a magical sign.

They had witches, too, both black and white. Some of the white witches were much venerated as clairvoyants and prophetesses. The black witches were feared as "The Night riders", who could fly, sometimes invisibly, and cast baneful spells.

The Saxons believed in many orders of elves and nature-spirits. At Lyminster, near Arundel, a deep and rather sinister pool is still called the Knucker Hole, a name derived from the Anglo-Saxon "Nicor", a water-demon. In modern times, Rudyard Kipling found that country people still believed in "the fairieses", a Sussex expression which he misheard as "Pharisees".

No doubt for a long time there were many people who followed the example of King Redwald of the East Saxons, who in the same temple had one Christian altar and another for the old gods.

All of these strands of belief, aboriginal, Celtic, Roman and Saxon, will have eventually made up the fabric of witchcraft. Christian persecution and banning, as I shall show further on, drove it underground and made it into a secret society.

As time went by, roads were driven through the great forest and over the heights of the Downs. Castles, towns and churches arose. Railways and factories followed them. Yet the old traditions are still there, for those who look for them. Right down to the present day, Sussex is one of the places where witchcraft lives.

- Doreen Valiente

Author's Acknowledgements

My grateful thanks are due to the staff of the Brighton Reference Library, for their courteous and untiring assistance.

Also to Mr. R. A. Kennedy of Brighton Museum, and Mr. N. E. S. Norris of Barbican House Museum, Lewes, for valuable assistance and information.

I must also thank Mr. Leslie Roberts, the well-known investigator of present-day black magic, for the loan of some rare books.

My thanks are also due to Mr. Francis Clive Ross, the former Editor of Light, for his permission to republish some material which first appeared in an article written by me in his magazine.

- Doreen Valiente

Who Witches Were

"Thus, I think, at first, a great part of philosophy was witchcraft"

- Sir Thomas Browne, Religio Medici, 1642.

Before we examine the records of Sussex witchcraft, either official or as preserved in folklore, let us enquire who witches really were. A brief look at the history of witchcraft in Britain may help the reader to get a clearer picture.

In the olden days every community had its witches. They were the doctors, midwives and practical psychologists of the common people. They also performed ceremonies to secure the fertility of the farmer's land and of his animals. They were the repositories of ancestral knowledge. Their secrets were guarded and handed down from generation to generation. On the darker side, their ill-will was feared. People took care not to offend them. The powers of the secret forces of nature were neutral. They could cure or kill.

Witches have existed ever since human society began. Sometimes they have been favoured by the government of the day, like the Sibyls of Ancient Rome. Sometimes they have been persecuted and had to live in hiding, like the Witch of Endor.

The word *"witch"* is thought to be derived from the same source as the words *"wit"* and *"wisdom"*, meaning *"a person with knowledge"*, Witchcraft is *"the craft of the wise"*. The Old English forms are *"wicca"* (masculine) and *"wicce"* (feminine), showing that a witch can be of either sex.

Modern research has found long names for the powers witches exercised: hypnotism, clairvoyance, mediumship, astral projection, extra-sensory perception, psycho-therapy. In olden times all these things came under one heading: witchcraft.

In Western Europe before the Christian era those who possessed unusual powers were often attached to the temples of the gods. With the coming of Christianity, however, the ancient mystery cults were forbidden and their followers were driven underground. But the common people still clung to the old seasonal festivals which to them were times of holiday; nor could they abandon the beliefs of centuries in one generation.

Moreover, the conversion of whole districts was often merely nominal. The king and his court might be baptised in order to please a powerful neighbour, like the King of Sussex was in A. D. 66 I. He and his chief ministers submitted to baptism in order to please the Christian King of Mercia, who was going to give him some land. But to the common people this meant little. Not until twenty years later did Wilfrid of York come to attempt the conversion of all Sussex.

The Church did what it could to combat old beliefs by giving them a new Christian form. For instance, the Roman feast of the Saturnalia and the old Saxon feast of Yule both of which took place in midwinter, became Christmas: Beltane, the beginning of May, became Roodmass. The midsummer feast, also called Beltane, became St. John's Day. Samhain Eve, when spirits were supposed to walk about, became All Saints' Eve, or Hallowe'en. The spring festival of the goddess *Eostre* or *Ostara* became Easter.

The old sacred places had Christian churches built upon them. Pagan sacred sites where suitable, were deliberately selected for this purpose. The reigning Pope in a letter to the Christian authorities in England advised them to do this because, he said, the people would go to the ancient sites anyway. If the Church tried to prevent them it would only make itself unpopular, so it was wiser to adapt than to destroy. Hence the older an English church is, the more likely is it to be built upon a pagan sacred place.

For many centuries the mass of the people continued to believe in the old pagan religion. This is shown by the meanings of the words *"pagan"* and *"heathen"* and their derivations. Both words have the sense of *"one who is not a Christian"*. The word *"pagan"* is from the Latin *paganus*, a peasant or rustic. The word *"heathen"* means *"one who lives on the heath"*, as opposed to a town-dweller.

The pagans and heathens still resorted to their old fertility rites, to their sibyls and charmers, their diviners and healers, the wise men and wise women, the witches. King Edgar legislated against heathenism in A. D. 959, and demanded its total extinction. King Canute in 1038 was demanding the same thing; probably with only a little more success than he had against the tide. Human nature is not to be changed by legislation.

Unfortunately this fact has never hindered legislators from the attempt. As the Church's influence became stronger the Church courts began to deal with witches as heretics. Their power to order executions varied with the temper of the rulers of the state at the time. For instance, when in 1324 in Ireland the Bishop of Ossory indicted Lady Alice Kyteler as a witch, he succeeded in having her waiting-woman Petronilla burned at the stake. Some of the nobility, however, opposed him, and Lady Alice herself was assisted to escape to England, where no further action seems to have been taken against her.

Increasing Church opposition eventually had the effect of driving witchcraft more and more underground. The old pagan rituals were held more and more in secret. Secret signs were instituted by which followers of the witches' beliefs could recognise one another. When newcomers were brought into the cult they were given a new name by which, and only by which, they were to be called at meetings. To use their real name was a misdemeanour. Witchcraft became a secret brotherhood.

> *Witches and warlocks, without any bother,*
> *Like gipsies, on meeting will know one another.*

The cult was organised into groups called covens. The word "*coven*" is actually a variant of the word "*convent*". The latter word was originally spelt and pronounced "*covent*", a form which remains in the name of Covent Garden. The Latinised spelling "*convent*" was introduced about 1550, and by about 1650 had superseded the Middle English form "*covent*". A "*coven*" or "*covent*" meant in particular a company of thirteen persons, twelve with a leader, who gathered together for some purpose, generally a religious one.

Chaucer in his Canterbury Tales makes one of his characters say, "*For threttene [thirteen] is a covent as I gesse*". A poem of the early fourteenth century called Handlyng Synne, a collection of cautionary tales, tells of a "*coveyne*" of thirteen people who held a dance in the churchyard while the priest was saying Mass, and how they were punished for their impiety. A book of Ecclesiastical Memorials written in 1536 speaks of "*All . . . houses of religion . . . whereof the number in anyone house is or of late hath been less than a covent, that is to say under 13 persons*".

As time went on the old word "*coven*" came to be used exclusively of the witches' cult group, though the latter could not always muster the full complement of thirteen. The chief male member of the coven was called the Devil, and the chief woman member the Maiden. There was also an Officer, whose job it was to summon the members to meetings.

Inevitably the witch cult became more and more clandestine and forbidden as the Church's power grew. The old traditional knowledge and beliefs became more and more fragmentary as covens were scattered. The Reformation in Britain brought for a time even fiercer persecution under the secular law than had been known before. Some of it was influenced . by political considerations, such as James the First's fear of the intrigues against him by his kinsman Earl Bothwell, who was a member of the witch cult. Some of it was fired by the Puritan zeal which banned the maypole and tried to abolish Christmas.

In 1542, under Henry VIII, an Act of Parliament was passed declaring witchcraft a felony. This Act was repealed under the next king, Edward VI. In 1563, under Elizabeth I, a new Act was passed which punished with death the consulting of evil spirits for any purpose, and all witchcraft which intended death. Witchcraft which caused bodily injury or harm to a person's goods, was punished by a year's imprisonment, which entailed exposure four times In the pillory, for a first offence, and by death for a second offence. Under James I in 1603 another new Act was passed by which all forms of witchcraft, black or white, were punishable by death. This continued to be the law until 1736, when it was repealed, and replaced by an Act which said that any person pretending to practise witchcraft should be punished by a year's imprisonment and four periods of exposure in the pillory. This Act continued to be the law until 1951. It was then repealed, and replaced by the Fraudulent Mediums Act.

On March 1st, 1956, the then Home Secretary Major Lloyd-George, stated in the House of Commons that "*the practice of black magic is an offence at common Law*", and that police action could be taken against it under the Fraudulent Mediums Act of 1951. His remarks were reported in The Times on March 2nd, 1956. However, to date no such prosecution has ever been brought.

When eighteenth-century humanism and rationalism finally put an end to the death penalty for witchcraft, few covens were left. Fragments of tradition had been handed down to individuals, who mingled them with Christian charms such as the "White Paternoster" and similar rhymes. They saw nothing incongruous in so doing. They were not theologians. They were just simple, unlettered folk who felt rather than consciously believed in the reality of timeless, unseen Powers, by whatever name those Powers might be called.

However much magic and religion were dissociated in the minds of the clergy, they were not so dissociated in the minds of the common people. Mrs. Charlotte Latham, writing in 1868 about Sussex superstitions, said:

> *"Persons who have been confirmed in their youth sometimes again present themselves for Confirmation in old age, because they think the Bishop's blessing will cure them of some bodily ailment. I have heard of an old woman who was confirmed several times because she thought it was good for her rheumatism."*
>
> - C. Latham

This is not such a far cry in fundamental belief from the wife of Edward Jones who in 1582 was summoned before the Ecclesiastical Court held by the Archdeacon of Lewes, on a charge of putting the Communion wafer into her glove and conveying it away instead of eating it. She was not, as sensational writers would allege, a "Satanist". She was merely trying to possess herself of something she believed to be a powerful magical object to use as a charm. Pevensey Church in Sussex still possesses an old font which is provided with a locked cover to prevent people stealing the holy water for use in spells.

Whatever the law, the Church, or the schoolmaster might say, the belief in witchcraft still continued. Indeed, it continues to this day. The white witch is still consulted. The black witch is still feared. Many beliefs held about witches are merely fantastic. But any belief, however fantastic, has to have a reason for its existence. I shall try in this book, to show what some of these reasons are.

The Horned God in Sussex

Laws against black magic go back to the beginnings of recorded history. By black magic is meant the use of occult powers for evil purposes. However, as we have seen, in time witchcraft in itself began to be banned by law, whether used for good purposes or bad ones.

The stand taken by the Church upon this subject was that all the old pagan gods were in fact demons or devils. Therefore anyone who invoked heathen gods, whether they meant harm to anyone or not, even if in fact they set out to cure, was a heretic and a devil worshipper.

An illustration of the beliefs of the early Church on this point may be found in one of the scenes carved on the wonderful old font in St. Nicholas' Church, Brighton. This font dates back to the early twelfth century, and among the carvings is a scene from the legendary life of St. Nicholas. This in itself shows that the legend was taken seriously in the days when the font was carved.

St. Nicholas is depicted defeating the magical wiles of none other than the goddess Diana. He was Bishop of Myra, a place where there was also a great temple to Diana. The Bishop led his followers to destroy Diana's temple. In revenge, the goddess, or as the early Christians believed, the demon who was worshipped as Diana, resolved to destroy the Christian church at Myra.

She made a flask of magical oil which would cause any building anointed with it to go up in flames. Then taking the shape of a nun, she appeared walking on the sea to a ship full of pilgrims who were going to Myra. The pilgrims took her for a sacred vision. When she gave them the flask and told them it was a precious ointment with which they were to anoint the walls of the church at Myra, they accepted it as a miraculous gift. However, St. Nicholas also appeared walking upon the water, to foil the demon, and ordered them to throw the flask into the sea. They did so, and the flask and Diana together disappeared in a blaze of flame.

The scene on the font, carved in the stiff Byzantine style, shows the pilgrim ship with the goddess-demon standing on the water on one side, proffering the magic flask. St. Nicholas with his bishop's crozier stands on the water on the other side, urging them to throw the devil's gift overboard.

With beliefs such as this seriously held about the ancient gods, it is understandable how witchcraft and "devil-worship" came to be classed together under the old English laws.

The traditional appearance of the Devil, with horns, hoofs and tail, is precisely that of the Great God Pan as depicted in ancient sculptures. Pan was one of the oldest of the Greek gods, older than the classical gods of Olympus. His horns are the primitive symbol of power and virility. The Romans called him Faunus or Silvanus, the god of the woods and fields. He was the god of shepherds and fanners, the ruler of all horned beasts. He was also invoked as the god of hunting, from his lordship of the woods. The Gauls, the Celtic inhabitants of what we now call France, in the Roman days also worshipped the Horned God, whom they called Cernunnos. To them he was ruler of the Underworld, the place where the souls of the dead went while they waited to be reincarnated on earth.

The belief in reincarnation is very old and widespread. Charles Godfrey Leland at the end of the last century found it still lingering among Italian peasants when he was collecting information about witchcraft in Italy. Incidentally, he found that the peasants called witchcraft La Vecchia Religione, "The Old Religion".

In the Caverne des Trois Frères, at Ariege, France, is a remarkable picture, which any old-time witch-hunter would have denounced instantly as depicting the god of the witch covens or his earthly representative, the male leader of a coven in his ritual disguise. Yet this picture is a cave-painting drawn by men of the Stone Age. It has been estimated as being at least nine thousand years old.

It depicts, with remarkable power considering the primitive artist who drew it, a dancing man masked in the skin and horns of a stag. He is evidently performing some magical rite.

During the recent excavations at Starr Carr in Yorkshire on the site of a Stone Age hunters' camp, archaeologists found remains of some of the actual horned masks used in these ancient magical rites. They consisted of twenty or more frontlets of the skulls of stags, with the antlers attached. The antlers had been cleverly hollowed out to reduce their weight for wearing on the head, and the parietal bones behind them had been perforated for attachment to a mask. The bones had been smoothed inside to rest easily on the head of the wearer.

At the time when these particular magical masks were being used Britain was still joined by a large land-bridge to northern Europe. The cult of the Horned God continued to flourish and ritual dances were still held in his honour, long after the arrival of Christianity. The Liber Poenitentialis of Theodore, Archbishop of Canterbury (A. D. 668-690), besides prescribing penances for witchcraft, says:

> *"If anyone at the Kalends of January goes about as a stag or a bull; that is, making himself into a wild animal and dressing in the skin of a herd animal, and putting on the heads of beasts; those who in such wise transform themselves into the appearance of a wild animal, penance for three years because this is devilish."*

> — Theodore, Archibishop of Canterbury AD 668-690

In spite of this and similar prohibitions, such: dances and rituals still held their place in British folk life. The famous Horn Dance of Abbot's Bromley, Staffordshire, I believe continues to this day. So does the Puck Fair at Killorglin in Ireland, where, amid scenes of much enthusiasm and a plentiful flow of whiskey, a billy-goat is solemnly crowned as King Puck.

[The mad pranks of Robin Goodfellow - Woodcut, 1682]

Now, this gives us a clue as to who the original Puck of Pook's Hill was, here in Sussex. He was none other than the old god of the woods himself, with all his traditional attributes. "*Puck*" or "*Pouke*" is an Old English word for the Devil. Yet it forms part of many Sussex place-names, such as Pookhill, Puckscroft, Puckstye, Pookreed, etc.

Puck was also known as Robin Goodfellow A woodcut illustrating an old chapbook called The Mad Pranks of Robin Goodfellow, dated 1628, shows him clearly in his character as the god of the witch-covens. Rough and crude as this old woodcut is, it is evident that it depicts a night dance of witches. The central figure is Puck himself, holding a broomstick in one hand and a lighted candle in the other. The coven, six men and six women placed alternately, dance around him in a ring, following a circle which is marked out upon the ground. Outside the circle are vessels holding food and drink, and a man playing music for the dancers. Owls flit through the night sky overhead. Seated outside the ring of dancers is an animal that looks like a witch's black cat.

The central figure of Puck or Robin Goodfellow is drawn larger than the rest, to emphasise its importance and place of honour. This is the coven's leader, the Devil, in his ritual disguise of horned mask and animal's hide. In spite of the crudeness of the woodcut, he is clearly a man disguised. He is naked to the waist. Below the waist he wears a costume of skins, and leggings which simulate cloven hoofs. On his head is a mask with horns and large pointed ears.

The broomstick he carries has a phallic significance in English folklore. In some parts it is thought unlucky for an unmarried girl to step over a broomstick, because if she does it is a sign that "*she will be a mother before she is a wife*". In Sussex in bygone days the maypole, itself a phallic symbol, used to be topped by a large birch broom.

Things that are sex symbols are life symbols, and hence lucky. This is the hidden meaning behind many objects which are traditional luck-bringers. It explains why, for instance, in old times a broomstick or besom was built into the walls of houses to bring luck to the inhabitants. In 1930, when alterations were being made to an old house in Blandford, Dorset, one such broomstick was found behind a wall- and carefully replaced. Anyone who has ever visited the ruins of Pompeii and other ancient towns and seen the phallic symbols placed on house walls as luck-bringers and averters of the Evil Eye will recognise the connection.

The witch's broomstick is a substitute for the old symbol of Priapus which used to be carried at pagan fertility festivals.

Proof that the chief male member of the witches' coven was called the Devil is found in an item in The Calendar of State Papers dated 1584. This gives a list of eighty-seven "suspected persons", among whom are *"Ould Birtles the great devil, Roger Birtles and his wife, and Anne Birtles"*, and a number of other people specified as witches.

With this meaning in mind, many apparently fantastic passages in the evidence given at witch-trials become clear. The idea probably was that as the god of the witches, the old Pan, Silvanus or Cernunnos was called by Churchmen the Devil, so his chief henchman took the name of the Devil too.

Let us return to those ritual remembrances of the Horned God which have continued to be a part of folk life right into modern times. Of these, one of the most interesting takes place annually in Sussex. It is the Horn Fair held every year at the village of Ebernoe on July 25th, St. James's Day.

It has some relation to the Horn Fair which used to be held at Charlton, Kent, because the old Sussex folk-song called the Horn Fair Song exactly describes what used to happen at Charlton, and a song very similar to it used to be sung at the Charlton Horn Fair also. The last verse of the Sussex song goes like this:

> *"O fairest of damsels, how can you say No?*
> *With you I intend to Horn Fair for to go.*
> *We'll join the best of company when we do get there,*
> *With horns on their heads, boys, the finest at the Fair. "*

No procession *"with horns on their heads"* is today held at Ebernoe, but it certainly used to be held at Charlton. Hone's Every-day Book says of it that :

> *". . . the procession of people with horns in their hats was*
> *accompanied by so many indecencies on Blackheath, such as the*
> *whipping of females with furze, that it gave rise to the proverb*
> *'All is fair at Horn Fair."*
> - Hone's Every-day Book

"The whipping of females with furze" will be recognised by anthropologists as being a very old and widespread fertility ritual. Mild whipping was thought to drive away evil influences and arouse the forces of life. A typical example of this custom was the Roman Lupercalia.

F. T. Elworthy, in his book Horns of Honour, tells us of Charlton Horn Fair that it was held on St. Luke's Day, October 18th. "On that day a procession, of which we have accounts dating back to 1598, used to start from Cuckolds' Point near Deptford, and march through Greenwich to Charlton. The riotous mob composing it used to wear harm of different kinds upon their heads; while, at the fair, rams' horns, gilded toys, and even gingerbread in the shape of horns, were sold. All kinds of licence and indecency used to be practised on Blackheath, whence the proverb *"All is fair at Horn Fair"*.

This procession was abolished in 1768, but the fair itself continued until 1872, when it was banned by the Home Secretary after local good folk had got up an agitation against it. One of them wrote to The Times, saying it was intolerable that *"this saturnalia is held by the side of a church"*. So the Charlton Horn Fair faded into the past, to join the Whitsun Ales, the May Day bowers, the Midsummer bonfires, and most of the rest of Merry England.

However, in the remote little Sussex village of Ebernoe the old Horn Fair had been revived in 1864, after a lapse of many years, and it has continued to this day. It is believed by local people to be of great antiquity. What it was like in olden times we have only the traditional Horn Fair song to tell us, but it is evident from the latter that it resembled the Charlton Horn Fair, at any rate in the procession of people with horns on their heads.

Today a horned sheep is roasted whole on a spit, with wool wound round the horns to protect them. It is said to be lucky to take a turn at basting the sheep, and visitors give a small donation for the privilege of doing this.

The village cricket team entertains a visiting team to a match, and the cricketers and their friends are the first to eat of the roasted sheep. After the match the batsman who has scored the highest number of runs is presented with the sheep's head and horns. This prize is highly valued, and is taken home to be cleaned and mounted. It is believed to bring fertility to its owner's land, and to ensure him a large and flourishing family. A bachelor who has won several pairs of horns is reported to have told someone to whom he showed them: *"I've pinned my hopes of finding a wife on these horns. When I'm married I shall expect a large family, too. "*

Whether he spoke in jest or earnest, it shows the beliefs held by local people as to the significance of Horn Fair. The people of nearby Kirdford believe in sowing their cabbages the day after Horn Fair to ensure a good crop. As I have said, unlettered country folk, whether of Christian or pre-Christian times, were not theologians. They did not trouble themselves with complicated dogmas. On the contrary, they accepted that things superhuman were by definition beyond human intellect. They concerned themselves with the things they saw around them, the forces of life, death and rebirth.

They saw the corn spring up afresh year after year, the trees put out new leaves every spring. They saw new life begotten and born. They saw old things wither and fade away. Of these things, of the fire on their hearths, the cattle in their byres, the beasts they hunted in the woods of the sun in the morning and the moon at night, their religion was made. Or rather, was not consciously made, but grew of itself out of the deep roots in the collective unconscious of humanity.

Of this primitive and instinctive desire for kinship with the forces of life, the cult of the Horned God was a part. This is why its memory has endured.

⚜

Sussex Witch Trials

The popular belief about the punishment of witches is that they were burned at the stake. This is true only for Scotland and the Continent and for England prior to the Reformation. In the reign of Edward I, a compendium of the laws of England as then existing said that the punishment of burning should be carried out *"upon sorcerers, sorceresses, renegades, sodomites, and heretics publicly convicted"*.

However, as we have seen, much depended upon the willingness of the secular authorities to carry out the extreme sentence, and in fact lighter sentences, such as exposure in the pillory or some similar form of penance, were often passed.

Witches were not always regarded with horror and execration. There is a case on record, for instance, where in 1570 the Vicar of St. Dunstan's, near Canterbury, made an indignant complaint to the authorities that the keeper of the gaol in Canterbury was allowing an imprisoned witch too much liberty. Further, the gaoler had publicly remarked that '*the witch did more good by her physic than Mr. Pundall and Mr. Wood being preachers of God's word.'*

After the Reformation, the secular law took precedence in England, and witches were executed, if sentenced to death, by hanging. The penalty of burning remained in Scotland as did the horrible practice of torture to extract confessions. This was not legal in England, though the foul gaols in which suspects were detained were a torture in themselves.

However, it is evident from the records of English witch trials that ill-treatment of various kinds, which did not legally rank as torture, was inflicted to extract confessions. This included starvation, deprivation of sleep by being forcibly walked up and down for hours on end, and *"swimming"*; that is, having the hands and feet bound together crosswise, and being flung into water, such as a deep pond, to see if the suspect sank or floated. If they floated, it was a sign of guilt. If they sank, they were hauled out by means of a rope which had been tied

25

about their waists, and adjudged not guilty. The effect of such an ordeal upon old and infirm people was sometimes fatal whether they sank or swam. The idea behind the swimming test seems to have been that as the witches had rejected their Christian baptism and turned to the service of the Devil, so the water would in turn reject them, and they would float as a sign of guilt.

A record exists in the archives of Rye, Sussex, that on December 7th, 1645, the Mayor and others issued an order for *"Martha, the wife of Stephen Bruff, and Anne Howsell, widow, being suspected to be witches, to be tried by putting them in the water"*.

It followed a complaint by Frances Royall, the wife of William Royall that Mrs. Howsell had come twice into her home in a supernatural manner. The first occasion, Mrs. Royall said, was about midnight one night, when she had heard a dog howling outside her street door. She looked out of the window and called out, but the dog would not go away. Then, without the door opening, Mrs. Howsell had entered the room and approached her bedside. She took her by the left hand and said,

"Goody Royall, you must go with me".

"Whither?" asked the frightened Mrs. Royall,

and the other replied "Home".

But she refused, and the spectral visitant vanished. Later she repeated her visit, this time coming through a pane of glass.

Such was the evidence upon which Anne Howsell was ordered to be swum. The evidence against Martha Bruff is not recorded. Mrs. Royall may have been dreaming, or the whole thing may have been a malicious invention on her part. However, it seems likely from the absence of any further record of trial or punishment that Anne Howsell and Martha Bruff were declared not guilty by the ordeal.

Many guesses have been made at the actual number of persons tried and condemned as witches in England. This question remained in the realm of guesswork, often sensational guesswork, until the researches of Mr. C. L'Estrange Ewen the results of which were published in his book *Witch Hunting and Witch Trials* in 1929. Mr. Ewen undertook the first systematic search of the public records to find and examine accounts of witch trials.

Reading his book, one feels admiration for his even undertaking such a task, let alone achieving successful results. He decided to concentrate first on the records for the Home Circuit of Assizes, comprising the counties of Essex, Hertfordshire, Kent, Surrey and Sussex, because these went the farthest back, commencing in 1559. He estimates that about 77 per cent of the Home Circuit records have survived. Of these, he found some well preserved, others crushed, crumpled, full of dust, and sometimes in the last stages of decay. Sometimes they were quite impossible to read. Other records were misplaced or wrongly labelled. Those that were legible were usually written in crabbed and abbreviated Latin, full of antiquated legal terms.

From this mass of mouldering documents, the determination and scholarship of Mr. Ewen have succeeded in giving us at least a good proportion of the facts about witch trials in England. He tells us, however, that his figures may only represent about half of the actual trials which took place in the Home Circuit. They do not include trials in towns judicially independent of the assizes; and trials by order of the municipal authorities, such as the one by the Mayor of Rye noted above, seem to have been fairly numerous.

Mr. Ewen went on to examine the records of the other Assize Circuits in England and Wales, but we can only concern ourselves here with his figures for Sussex. He states that seventeen persons are shown as being indicted for witchcraft in Sussex between the years covered by the Home Circuit records, between 1558 and 1736. However, counting the cases in his abstracts of indictments I can only find sixteen, of which two evidently refer to the same person, making fifteen persons indicted in all. Of these fifteen persons, only four were convicted, and of these four only one was sentenced to death.

This is actually the lowest figure for the five counties of the Home Circuit, and contrasts with the hideous total of eighty-two hangings in Essex, which has the highest figures of hangings and indictments. Sussex people seem to have shown a greater degree of toleration than existed in other places in England, as the belief in witchcraft was universal in those times.

Here in brief are the sixteen cases from Sussex:

1572. At East Grinstead Assizes, Joan Usbarne of Hailsham, the wife of John Usbarne, husbandman, was accused of bewitching to death a bull and a cow.

1575. At East Grinstead Assizes, Margaret Cooper of Kirdford, the wife of William Cooper, surgeon, was accused of bewitching to death two men and a woman.

1577. At Horsham Assizes, Margery Barrow of Chailey, spinster, was accused of bewitching a woman. Juliana Curtis of Crawley, spinster, was accused of bewitching a woman. Alice Casselowe of Mayfield, spinster, was accused of bewitching to death an ox and two pigs.

1579. At Horsham Assizes, Alice Stedman of Stedham, the wife of John Stedman, a "woodbrooker" (? woodbroker), was accused of bewitching three cows and a steer, and causing the cows to calve prematurely.

1580. At East Grinstead Assizes, Ursula Welfare of Alfriston, spinster, was accused of bewitching to death a sow, eight chickens, and two hens at Alfriston, and two oxen at Berwick.

1589. At East Grinstead Assizes, Edward Roydon of Hailsham, a glover, was accused of bewitching to death a cow and a mare, of bewitching two men so that one of them lost the use of his right arm, and of bewitching another man to death.

1591. At East Grinstead Assizes, Agnes Mowser of Fletching, spinster, was accused of bewitching a young woman.

1593. East Grinstead Assizes, Elizabeth Whighte of Balcombe, spinster, was accused of bewitching four persons, two men and two women.

1602. At Horsham Assizes, Robert Stockton of Dallington, a labourer, was accused of bewitching a man to death.

1605. At East Grinstead Assizes, Robert Stikden of Dallington, a chandler (probably the same person as the above), was accused of bewitching a woman.

1617. At East Grinstead Assizes, Margaret Pannell of Salehurst, wife of Thomas Pannell, was accused of bewitching a man and a woman so that they were "wasted and consumed", and of bewitching to death a sow and eight pigs.

1654. At Horsham Assizes, Jane Shoebridge of Withiam, spinster, was accused of bewitching a twelve year old girl. Clement Shoebridge of Withiam, a widow, was accused of bewitching a man, and also of bewitching on a later occasion the same young girl that Jane Shoebridge was accused of troubling, all the alleged victims being stated to be "wasted and consumed".

1680. At Horsham Assizes, Alice Nash of Battle, the wife of Thomas Nash, a labourer, was accused of bewitching to death two little girls.

- C. L'Estrange Ewen, based upon Home Circuit records, 1558-1736

Only four people of the above were found guilty, namely Joan Usbarne in 1572, who was sentenced to one year's imprisonment; Margaret Cooper in 1575, who was sentenced to death by hanging; Alice Casselowe in 1577, who was sentenced to a year's imprisonment and died in prison; and Agnes Mowser in 1591, who was sentenced to a year's imprisonment. Sentences of one year's imprisonment always carried with them four periods of six hours each in the pillory.

There are no records of witch trials at the Lewes Assizes; but in the Act Books of the Archdeaconry Court of Lewes we find an account of a trial of two women from Hove on a charge of witchcraft. On May 21st 1588, Margery Banger, a widow, and her daughter Joane were cited for being *"vehemently suspected to be notorious witches and common practisers of the same"*. The widow Margery appeared before the court and denied the charge. On June 4th 1588, John Bradford of Hove was presented before the court for being *"a great manteyer (?maintainer) of Margery and Joane Banger in their witchcraft"*.

The court ordered a trial by compurgation. That is, the accused were ordered to find four persons of good character who were prepared to swear that they were innocent of the charge. Four women, Joane Bradford, Margaret Burton, Elizabeth Collen of Brighthelmstone, and Joane Alley of Hove, were found willing to do this. As a result, on June 18th, 1588, Joane and Margery Banger were held to have sufficiently cleared themselves of the charge of witchcraft.

One other Lewes case may be noted. In 1578 a man called Tree, a bailiff of Lewes, and another man called Smith, of Chinting, were ordered *"to be examined touching conjuration"*. In other words, they were suspected of practising magic.

It is significant that they are not described as witches. There is a very recognisable difference between ceremonial magic and witchcraft. The former is the kind of magic contained in the Grimoires, such as The Key of Solomon, The Grand Grimoire, The Grimorium Verum, or the Lemegeton. It is a tradition which derives for the greater part from the Hebrew Cabala, which in its turn is the Secret Tradition of Israel, and possibly stems originally from Ancient Egypt in its basic concepts.

Scholars of the Middle Ages and the Renaissance realised that the Jews possessed secret magical knowledge. So they studied Hebrew, ostensibly for the purpose of converting the Jews, but actually to learn their secrets. Then they translated the Cabalistic knowledge into Latin or their own language, and sometimes gave the original rituals a veneer of Christianity.

Ceremonial magic, therefore, is a tradition of scholars and sometimes of priests. Its basic idea is to conjure and control spirits by invoking the secret and powerful Names of God, the *"Words of Power"* which King Solomon knew. Certain basic beliefs are common to both witchcraft and ceremonial magic; but witchcraft is more primitive, simple and direct, and connects back to pagan fertility cults of great antiquity. It is a thing of the countryside, whereas ceremonial magic is a thing of the study and the secret sanctuary. The ceremonial magician has to be something of a scholar, whereas the witch may be completely illiterate.

It is important to recognise the different streams of occult tradition. Some writers, notably Montague Summers, tend to lump together both ceremonial magic and witchcraft, and to ascribe them both to the deliberate invocation of Satan. This sweeping generalisation is quite misleading, but unfortunately is often accepted.

The distinction between ceremonial magic and witchcraft was usually made and understood by our ancestors. The two Lewes men referred to above were ordered *"to be examined touching conjuration"*; but in the previous year, 1577, Joan à Wood was presented before the Sessions of the Peace at Seaford, Sussex, *"for being a witch"*.

Two Strange Stories

A witch trial that took place at Rye, Sussex, in 1607 is so curious that it deserves to be considered on its own. It concerns two women, Mrs. Anna or Ann Taylor and Mrs. Susanna Swapper, who lived next door to each other in Lion Street, one of the picturesque little streets of the old seaport town.

The houses in which they lived belonged to old Mrs. Bennett, Ann Taylor's mother. She was locally supposed to be something of a wise woman, or white witch, and was consulted by her neighbours for the cure of illnesses. Ann Taylor's husband George is described as a gentleman. The Swappers, Roger and Susanna, were of humbler station and rented their house from Mrs. Bennett. Roger Swapper was a sawyer.

In 1607 Susanna Swapper and Ann Taylor were denounced as witches. Susanna was brought before the Mayor, Thomas Higgons, to be questioned, and her statements were taken down by the Town Clerk.

She said that it all started one night when at about midnight, as she was lying in bed, she saw four spirits appear to her. One of them was a tall, clean-shaven young man dressed in a white surplice, who gave his name as Richard. Another was an older man with a grey beard, who was clothed in white with a satin doublet and pinked breeches; he gave the name of Robert. Then there were two women, Catherine and Margery, one of whom was dressed in a green petticoat and a white waistcoat, and the other all in white.

The next day she told her friend Mrs. Taylor about the apparition, and Mrs. Taylor said it was an illusion. However, the spirits appeared twice more, so she told Mrs. Taylor again, and she advised her to ask the spirits what they wanted. The next time they appeared she did so, and they told her to go to Ann Bennett (Mrs. Taylor) and call her into the garden to dig.

Ann and Susanna accordingly went into the garden, with Ann's thoughts at least on buried treasure. However, one of them felt ill, probably with fright or excitement, so they did not continue long. Ann Taylor told Susanna that the previous occupant of her house, one Roger Pyewall, had also been troubled by spirits, and been told to dig in the garden; but he was so afraid of the affair that he would not do it, and had since died.

Ann said that she was heir to the money, and promised the Swappers that if they could find out from the spirits where the money was buried they should have a hundred pounds for themselves, and should never want.

The spirits confirmed that money was buried in the garden, and mentioned another recent find of buried treasure at a place called Weeks Green, which Ann Taylor had heard of.

The spirit Richard, who was Susanna's chief communicator, eventually, persuaded Susanna to go to Weeks Green. What followed is told in the words of Susanna's deposition, which is preserved on a single sheet among the Harleian MSS., No. 358, Art. 47. Fol. 188. I have modernised the spelling:

> *"And she did learn the way of Ann Bennett (Ann Taylor), and did go thither, and there did see the tall man (Richard) stand in the street; and he called her to follow him through a rye field into the green field next to it, which she did; and in the middle of the field there was a valley of the one side, and a bank on the other; and there he told her in that valley there was a pot and gold in it, and a chain upon the top of it; and beside the pit, under I little stub, there was a crock, metal, with three legs, in which there was money. And he bade her sit down upon a bank, which she did; and then she saw a man, all in black, on the one side of the hedge; and a woman in green on the same side, going to meet one another. And she thought the ground did move under her as she sat; and then she cried, 'Lord have mercy upon me, what shall become of me?' And then the tall man came to her again, and bade her be not afraid, for she should have no harm and seeing the two persons before mentioned, she asked the tall man what they were. And he said, 'The woman is Queen of the Fairies', and that if she would kneel to her she would give her a living; and then she looked and they were gone. And the tall man*

came to her again, and willed her to arise and go home; but she could not arise; and he willed her in the name of God to arise. And then she arose and went home sick to bed, and the man vanished away."

- Harleian MSS., No. 358

The curious point about this story is the reference to the Queen of the Fairies. This was a term used of the Maiden of a witch coven. In Scotland she was called the Queen of Elphame, and in France the Queen of the Sabbat. The man all in black who appeared with her may well have been the Devil of a coven, who is often described like this. Were all these appearances purely visionary, or were flesh and blood people involved? It is hard to say.

Susanna said that she had seen at various times eighteen spirits, but only the first four she saw, Richard, Robert, Catherine and Margery, ever spoke to her. But Ann Taylor told her that she had seen eighty or a hundred spirits, *"and they were all fairies"*. What she meant by this is uncertain; whether she was trying to tell Susanna that she too could see spirits, or whether she was referring to the very old folk belief that part at least of the fairy host was composed of the souls of people who had never been baptised, that is, were not Christians; among whom, of course, would be many followers of the Old Religion.

Sometimes spirits or visionary pictures would appear in the glass of a window, and both George and Ann Taylor saw them there. Susanna said that these visions were sent to convince them, because of their unbelief. Susanna was in the habit of laying flowers and herbs in the windows where the spirits were wont to appear, also water, bread and meat at various times, which the spirits caused to disappear, presumably as a test of their powers. She also saw the spirit Richard walking in the town at various times, and once Robert is mentioned thus also.

All this must have made very strange hearing to the Mayor and Jurats of Rye. Ann Taylor and Susanna Swapper were arrested and lodged in Rye Gaol, accused of consulting with evil spirits. They were tried at the General Sessions at Rye and condemned to death.

There are signs of a private grudge against Ann Taylor being held by Martha, who became the wife of Thomas Higgons, the Mayor who tried the case. Ann Taylor had commented on this lady's morals, accusing her of associating with her first husband, Thomas Hamon, the previous Mayor, before their marriage and while his first wife was still alive. She had also remarked on her marrying Higgons within three weeks of Hamon's death. In return, Martha now gave evidence that she believed Ann Taylor had bewitched Hamon to death.

George Taylor, Ann's husband, appealed to Sir John Boys, who intervened with the Mayor to cast doubt upon the court's legal right to try such a case. A stay of execution was secured, apparently with a view to a retrial. However, the Mayor refused to release Ann Taylor on bail, and she remained imprisoned in the Ypres Tower. George Taylor then appealed to the Lord Warden of the Cinque Ports, the Earl of Northampton. In his petition he stated that his wife was *"now with child, and grown very weak by reason thereof and the loathsomeness of the prison"*.

The Lord Warden sent a very sharp memorandum to the Mayor of Rye, in which he said that Ann Taylor was being kept in the common gaol *"upon the unjust accusation of a lewd woman and some private displeasure conceived by yourself against her"*.

The Mayor replied that Ann had been convicted for aiding and abetting Susanna Swapper in witchcraft. Her husband had promised that she would appear before the court when called on, but she had run away for half a year into Kent. She had returned to Rye secretly, and had been apprehended after a quarrel with her maid-servant, and lodged in gaol. Nevertheless, the Mayor agreed to bail her in her husband's surety of £100.

The matter dragged on until 1611, when the case was again laid before the town's legal advisers, who concurred in the opinion that it was covered by the general pardon. The Mayor, Thomas Higgons, who started the case, had died, and after the Lord Warden's intervention they were probably glad to be rid of it. Ann and Susanna were cleared accordingly.

Another strange Sussex story concerns what are known nowadays as poltergeist phenomena. At the time it took place, around 1662, all such things were put down to witchcraft. However, in modern days psychical research has devoted much time to the study of such occurrences, and reached certain tentative conclusions about them.

For one thing, it has been noticed that such phenomena are often associated with the presence in the household where they occur of adolescents or children. Young people passing through the psychic stresses associated with puberty seem sometimes to act as the focus of such disturbances. Sometimes, too, but less frequently, neurotic adults can become the centre from which the phenomena seem to draw their power to manifest.

The phenomena themselves are often characterised by a senseless, aggressive destructiveness. Stones are thrown by an invisible agency. Knockings and strange noises disturb the household. Furniture and crockery are thrown about. Sometimes fires start spontaneously. Sometimes weird forms are seen. The phenomena vary in strength from the mildly odd to the terrifying and dangerous. Psychic researchers still do not know the full answer to the problem of these strange occurrences.

The following story is contained in the MS. collections relating to Sussex left by the Rev. W. Hayley, rector of Brightling, to the British Museum. The date of about 1662 is indicated by the names mentioned. I have modernised the spelling and punctuation:

"   *At Brightling, in Sussex.*
As touching the relation of the Brightling Story, which is in substance undoubtedly true, however some circumstances of it may vary, be pleased to take the following account.
On Monday was three weeks (ago) at or near the house of Joseph Cruttenden, of Brightling, an old woman about noon came to a servant girl of the said Cruttenden's and tells her sad calamities were coming upon her master and dame; their house should be fired, and many other troubles befall them; but tells this girl withal, that if she spake of what she had told her, the Devil would tear her to pieces; otherwise she need not fear, for no hurt should come to her.
The same night, as the man and woman lay in bed, dirt and dust was thrown at them, but they could not tell whence it came. They rise and pray, during which the disturbances cease. Some say they went to bed again, but finding the same trouble they are forced to rise. Tuesday, about noon, dust and dirt, and several things are thrown at them again; before night, a part of one end of their house fired; they rake it down, it flashes somewhat like gunpowder; as they stopped it there, it began in another place,

and then in another, till the whole house was burnt down. Some say something like a black bull was seen tumbling about; the certainty of which I aver not. The house, though it burned down to the ground, it flamed not. The night was spent in carrying away goods, or one thing or another, to one place or another, they I think remaining most without doors. Thursday Colonel Busbridge (whose house the former was, being acquainted with the man's sad accident), bid them go into another of his houses in the parish, whither, when the goods were brought, such like disturbances were there also; the house fireth, endeavours are made by many to quench it, but in vain, till the goods are thrown out, when it ceased with little or no help.

In this condition none durst let them into their doors; they abide under a hut; the goods are thrown upside down; pewter dishes, knives, brick-bats strike them, but hurt them not. Mr. Bennett and Mr. Bradshaw, ministers, came to pray with them, when a knife glanced by the breast of Mr. Bennett, a bowl or dish (was) thrown at his back, but while at prayers quiet. They were without doors, there being very many present, a wooden tut (a kind of ladle) came flying out of the air, by many, and came and struck the man; as likewise a horseshoe, which was by some laid away, and it was observed of its own accord to rise again and fly to the man, and struck him in the midst of a hundred people.

Upon strict examination the man confesseth that he had been a thief, and did it under the colour of religion, (on the) Sabbath day. The girl told her dame the former story of the woman's discourse; she is sent for and examined before Capt. Collins and Mr. Busbridge, and she is watched and searched twenty-four hours; the girl says she is like the woman, but I think will not swear it is the same. This woman was formerly suspected to be a witch, had to go to Maidstone about it, but got away, and hath lived about Burwash some time since; her name I know not. Tuesday four ministers kept a fast, Mr. Bennett, Weller, Bradshaw and Golden. Since I hear not of any trouble. 'Tis said that they (the Cruttendens) are in a barn or alehouse. While they lay without doors, the woman sending some meal to a neighbour's to make some bread, they could not make it up into loaves, but it was like butter, and so they put it into the oven, but it would not bake, but came out as it went in.

- This relation came from Mr. Collins, who was an eyewitness to much of it.

- Rev. W. Hayley, Brightling Rector. 1662

The reader will note the presence of the young maid servant in this troubled family. They had only her word for it that the woman who was suspected of causing the trouble by witchcraft ever came to the door at all. However, this was sufficient to cause the woman to be *"watched and searched twenty-four hours"*. From what we know of witchhunting practices, this meant that she was imprisoned and deprived of food and sleep for that period, in the hope that her familiar spirits would contact her. Sometimes the suspect was made to sit cross-legged and bound so if necessary, upon a stool or table in the middle of the room, for hours on end. If during the time that she was being watched any animal, bird or even insect entered the room it would be killed on sight on suspicion of being one of her imps.

She would also be stripped and searched for the Devil's mark, with which he was supposed to brand his devotees. The description of this mark was so vague that it would fit almost any birthmark or small blemish, if the accusers wished it to. Sometimes the mark was supposed to be a spot insensitive to pain, which was searched for with long pins, while the suspect was blindfolded. Actually, it is quite possible to drive a sharp needle into the less sensitive parts of the body and yet cause very little feeling. Doctors make use of this fact today when giving hypodermic injections. The really determined witch-hunter had thus a fairly wide choice of means to secure a conviction.

The centre of interest for modern psychic researchers would have been that maid servant. Did she enjoy the drama of the examination of the suspected witch? Did she fake the phenomena, or did they happen because of her yet without her conscious volition? No further record has survived to tell us the end of this strange story.

Witches, Hares and the Moon

One of the most widespread Sussex beliefs about witches is that they possess the power to turn themselves into hares, especially at night. On summer nights when their bedroom windows were open old Sussex people used to lay a scythe blade across the sill with the sharp edge uppermost, as a charm to keep out the witch-hares who ran by night. A valley near Willingdon Hill, Sussex, bears the old name of Harewitch Bottom.

Mr. George Aitchison in Sussex Notes and Queries for May 1933 tells of his conversation in a West Sussex village with an old man who firmly believed in witchcraft, and who told him that he himself had known a witch in that very village. He believed that by means of her witchcraft she had plagued a certain farmer's animals.

"She had a book of charms, we all know, and she used it," he said. "But one of her daughters took it out of the village, and a good thing, too!"

The old man told Mr. Aitchison how one night he went to fetch help for a sick person. It was very late at night, when by a hedge he saw the dark form of a woman, whom he recognised as the witch.

"Why, Mrs. ___, he said, you ain't no call to be out so late as this!"

The form immediately vanished, and instead he saw a hare running through a gap in the hedge.

"I shall never forget it, he said, "not to my dying day!"

This old man had never been more than a day's walk from his own village, and knew nothing of stories in books about witches turning into hares.

A lady called Old Mother Digby of East Harting, was noted for her escapades in the shape of a hare. So also was a witch who used to live on Ditchling Common in a cottage called "Jack o' Spades". There are a number of Sussex stories about hunters whose dogs pursue a hare for a long and difficult chase; finally the hare leaps into a cottage garden or through a window for shelter. When the hunters arrive, there is no hare to be found. There is no one there but the lady of the house, in a dishevelled state as if she has been running!

This belief is by no means confined to Sussex. It is found all over Europe. We must therefore try to discover its possible origins.

The hare is often connected in mythology and folklore with the moon. The markings on the face of the full moon are widely believed to represent a hare. Hence the hare frequently appears as a servant of the Moon-goddess.

From very ancient times in Britain hares have been regarded as uncanny animals. Julius Caesar noted that the Ancient Britons were not permitted to eat hares, chicken or geese, but kept these creatures for pleasure. A prejudice against eating hare's flesh lingered among the country folk of the south-west parts of England as late as the nineteenth century, as it did also in parts of Wales, Ireland and Brittany. An exception was made of hare's brains, which were cooked and given to babies as a sedative.

To have a hare cross the road in front of anyone who was going on a journey or an errand was considered very unlucky. Anyone who saw such an omen was advised to turn back and postpone their business until the next meal had been eaten.

Sussex fishermen abominated hares and rabbits, which were usually classed with hares in folk belief. The very name of the creatures must not be mentioned when they were preparing their gear, or ill luck would attend their fishing. I have heard of people who wished to bring annoyance to another fisherman going secretly by night and nailing a hare's or rabbit's skin to the mast of his boat. They knew that as soon as the hateful skin was discovered the boat would have to be abandoned until it was thoroughly cleansed.

In the village of Glynde, Sussex, there is an old superstition that the word *"Hares"* must be said very loudly to oneself as the last word when retiring to rest on the last day of the month. On the following morning, the new month, one's first word must be *"Rabbits"*, also said loudly. This practice is thought to bring good luck for the month.

Now, the things mentioned in the superstitions detailed above, apart from the general uncanniness of the hare, are babies, the sea and the month. All three of these things, according to ancient lore, are ruled by the moon. It has often been said that in superstitions we can trace the remains of former religious beliefs, and the superstitions about hares are a case in point.

Hares, then, were the special creatures of the Moon-Goddess, and the association of witches with hares is a folk-memory of the fact that witches have been associated with the Moon-Goddess, as well as the Horned God, from time immemorial.

Shakespeare recognises this fact when he makes his three witches in Macbeth worshippers of Hecate, the ancient Greek Moon-Goddess of witchcraft. There is no mention of devil-worship or invocations of Satan in Shakespeare's representation of witchcraft. He knew that witches worshipped a Moon-Goddess, and represented them accordingly.

This is borne out by the fact that at the end of the nineteenth century investigations into witchcraft in Italy, where it is known as "*La Vecchia Religione*", or "*The Old Religion*", by Charles Godfrey Leland and others, disclosed the fact that Italian witches still worshipped the Moon-Goddess Diana and her daughter Aradia. In fact, I am told, the Old Religion still survives in Italy to this day.

We find many mentions of the goddess of the witches in mediaeval and later literature, and edicts of the Canon Law of the Church dating back to the ninth century A. D. have denounced those who followed her. The old Church edict known as the Canon Episcopi states:

> "*Some wicked women, perverted by the Devil, seduced by the illusions and phantasms of demons, believe and profess themselves in the hours of the night to ride upon certain beasts with Diana, the goddess of pagans, or with Herodias, and an innumerable multitude of women, and in the silence of the dead of night to traverse great spaces of earth, and to obey her commands as of their mistress, and to be summoned to her service on certain nights.*"
> - Canon Episcopi C9th AD

John of Salisbury, writing in the twelfth century A. D., tells of witches who hold feasts presided over by Herodias. The witches' Sabbats were known as *"the play of Diana"*, and Jerome Cardan in his book De Rerum Varietate, published in 1557, says:

> *"They (witches) adore the ludi Dominam (the Lady of the games) and sacrifice to her as a God."*
>
> - J. Cardan 1557

Other names for the witch goddess are Dame Habonde, Abundia, Satia, Bensozia, Zobiana, and Herodiana. In Scotland she was known as Nicneven, and the old poets write about her flying through the night air on Hallowe'en. In time the old pagan goddess dwindled in status to the Queen of the Fairies, or the Queen of Elphame, and the Maiden of a coven was given the name of the goddess and also known as the Queen of Elphame, as we have seen.

The Italian Aradia is evidently Herodias, and an Italian writer Pipernus writing about the witch cult in 1647 conjectured that the name did not refer to the character in the New Testament, but was much older. The nineteenth century American folklorist Charles Godfrey Leland agreed with this, and states his belief that the name Herodias was originally a title of Lilith, the weird Sumerian goddess of witchcraft and the Other World. The Jews had a lively belief in Lilith and made amulets to protect themselves against her as late as the Middle Ages. They had a legend that she had secretly lain with Adam before Eve was created, and by him had become the mother of the races of the fairies and the djinn, the non-humans who invisibly share this earth with his human descendants. She is the archetype of the primordial witch.

The *"certain nights"* on which the Canon Episcopi describes the witches as being summoned to the service of their pagan divinities would be the four Great Sabbats of Candlemas (February 2nd), May Eve or Walpurgis Night (April 30th), Lammas (August 1st), and Hallowe'en (October 31st). The lesser meetings, called Esbats, were held every full moon.

These old *"cross-quarter-days"*, as they were called, of the four Great Sabbats have their origin lost in antiquity. It has been surmised that they have something to do with the breeding season of cattle and wild creatures. We know that the Celts, the inhabitants of Britain and much of Europe before the spread of the Roman Empire, divided their year by them. The feast at the beginning of February they called Oimelc, the beginning of May was Beltane, the beginning of August was Lughnassad, and the beginning of November was Samhain. These occasions were celebrated by open-air rituals which usually involved a bonfire. This, incidentally, is the real origin of our *"Guy Fawkes Night"* on November 5th, so rousingly observed in Lewes and by many other Bonfire Societies in Sussex towns and villages.

Witchcraft is closely connected with the old fertility cult, magic to bring good luck to crops and cattle, and it is a very old belief that crops should be *"planted by the moon"*. That is, root crops should be planted in the dark of the moon, but crops which produce above ground should be planted in the waxing moon. Trees should be grafted or pruned in the moon's increase; but timber should be cut in the dark of the moon. Seeds intended for preservation should be gathered at new moon. Weeds should be grubbed up or cut down in the dark of the moon; then they are less likely to grow again.

It is believed that if a cow is taken to the bull in the waxing moon, her calf will be a bull-calf; if in the waning moon, it will be a cow calf. Cows are said to wish most strongly for the bull in the first and third quarters of the moon. Animals should only be castrated in the waning moon. Giving birth in animals and humans, will be easier if it happens at full moon.

These and other beliefs about the influence of the moon will originally have been associated with the Moon-goddess. Hence her importance in a fertility cult.

It is a matter of common knowledge that moonlight has a sexually stimulating and exciting effect upon human beings. The moon-goddesses of ancient times were also love-goddesses, often worshipped by orgiastic rites, and the concept of Diana as a chaste huntress is a very late one.

The old Sussex ritual of invoking the moon to obtain a vision of one's destined lover goes back to the belief in the love-goddess of the moon. This is how the ritual is worked: if a girl wishes to see a vision, or *"shim"* as it is called in Sussex dialect of her future husband, then at the first new moon that is visible after New Year's Day she must go out alone, without telling anyone, and sit across a gate or stile. She must look steadfastly at the moon and say to her:

"All hail to thee, moon! All hail to thee! I pray thee, good moon, reveal to me This night who my husband must be. "

She will then see a phantom appearance of her future husband.

Another clear relic of moon-worship is the belief that you should not see the new moon through a pane of glass. You should be out in the open and should bow or curtsey to "Lady Moon" for luck and turn your silver money in your pocket or purse. Silver is the metal of the moon.

In 1952 an article in the magazine Illustrated told of a shepherd at Steyning, Sussex who protected his flocks by making ritual observances to the moon from within *"fairy rings"*. When someone questioned him about these practices, he replied bluntly, *"Anyone would be a damn fool if he didn't"*.

Moon-magic played a big part in the healing activities of white witchcraft. For instance sufferers from scrofulous complaints could be much helped by fixing their eyes on the new May moon, and at the same time being presented with a box of ointment made from herbs gathered when the moon was full. Mrs. Charlotte Latham writing in 1868 about old Sussex beliefs tells how a man she knew living near Chichester took his grandchild to a *"cunning man"* in Dorset to be cured. When he arrived, he found upwards of two hundred persons waiting to have the healing ritual performed. As the new moon was not expected to rise before two o'clock in the morning they sat up all night to await the right moment.

If a theory held by the late Eliot Curwen, the well-known Sussex archaeologist, is correct, then the Barbican House Museum in Lewes contains evidence of the worship of the Moon-goddess in Sussex in the Stone Age.

In the Eliot Curwen Collection of Sussex flint implements on display in this museum are a number of curious objects which are tentatively described as *"horned scrapers"*. These are flints carefully chipped into a crescent or horned shape. They vary in the skill of their execution, but

43

in the better made ones the intention to represent a crescent is unmistakable. There seems to be little or no reason why a mere tool should have been made like this. Mr. Curwen observed that the convex side of the crescent was often pointed as if for mounting on a staff. So mounted, it would have formed a ritual wand and may have been used as a symbol of the Moon-goddess.

The moon symbol of the crescent persists today as the lucky horseshoe, so often displayed on old cottages to protect the inhabitants from witchcraft and the Evil Eye; a case of fighting witches with their own symbol, or appealing against black witchcraft to the goddess of witches herself. It is said that the horseshoe must be nailed with the points upwards, "*or the luck will run out*". Actually, this is to emphasise the crescent shape wherein the luck consists.

Donkey or pony shoes are also used as charms to avert misfortune from the household, being kept indoors on the mantelpiece. Sometimes these little shoes, more suitable for the cottage mantelpiece than the full-size horseshoe, have been silvered by being carefully covered with metal foil, to make them the moon's colour.

The Powers of Witchcraft

We have seen that two of the most ancient and widespread beliefs about witches are that they can fly by night, and that they can change their shape into that of a hare. There are more implications to these beliefs than the connection with the Moon-Goddess already discussed.

Modern psychic research has familiarised many of us with the term *"astral projection"*. By this is meant the projection of a non-material double of ourselves, sometimes called the *"astral body"*, to a distance from the physical body, which is usually in a state of sleep or trance at the time. The consciousness is more or less transferred to this non-material body, so that sometimes on waking from the trance we can describe places and incidents perceived at a distance.

This belief, with its necessary postulate that we possess such a non-material body in addition to our physical one, la actually one of the oldest in the world. The Ancient Egyptians, for instance, called the non-material body the Ka. The people of the East, the Hindus, Tibetans and Chinese, have always had words in their languages to describe the human double and its powers of action at a distance.

Today such bodies as the Society for Psychical Research have accumulated many accounts of these phenomena. Now we have come to realise that matter and energy are interchangeable terms, the idea that energy can manifest in many different states need not seem so strange to us.

What modern psychical researchers are beginning to investigate, country people have believed in for centuries. The word they use for the human double is the *"fetch"*. Witches, among other powers, possess that of sending their fetch to a distance, sometimes in their own shape and sometimes in that of an animal. It will be remembered how in Rye in 1645 Mrs. Royall claimed to be troubled by the *"fetch"* of Anne Howsell, and how Mrs. Howsell, was ordered to be swum for a witch in consequence.

It was the witch's fetch which ran the countryside by night in the form of a hare. Sometimes too, people believed it to take the form of a cat, another animal formerly sacred to the Moon-goddess. Dorothy Sayers wrote an effective short story, The Cyprian Cat, around this belief. In this story, someone shoots the witch-cat, and the witch herself is found dying from a bullet-wound. The usual belief, however, was that the fetch in animal form was immune to anything but a silver bullet. This idea explains the other old belief that a witch or a magician casts no shadow as they walk. What is walking is not the person in bodily form but their fetch and, of course, this would cast no shadow.

In stories of Italian witches the idea emerges clearly. We are told that at midnight they strip naked and rub themselves all over with an unguent made of certain herbs, repeating an incantation to be carried wherever they will to go. Then they lie down and pass into a trance and their spirits quit their bodies, coming out of their mouths like a vapour, which takes the shape of a bat and flies away. Before dawn the spirits come fluttering back and re-enter their bodies again, and the witches regain consciousness and sit up.

There are many accounts of experiments conducted by the more intelligent investigators of witchcraft in olden times with the Witches' Salve, as the trance-inducing unguent was called. Jerome Cardan, for instance, tells us how he experimented with the salve, after witches had told him remarkable stories of their visions under its influence. He says that it caused him to sleep and to see joyful dreams. Other stories tell of witches who rubbed themselves all over with the salve, and passed into a profound trance. Sometimes on regaining consciousness they were able to describe events at a distance. Sometimes they gave wild accounts of erotic revels they had been taking part in at the Sabbat.

The writers against witchcraft gave lurid accounts of how witches violated graves and murdered children to obtain human fat with which to compound their vile concoction. This, however, was probably mere propaganda. Any oil or fat would make a medium for the herbs. Herbalists usually made their unguents with hog's lard.

With regard to the herbs themselves, it seems that substances which if taken by the mouth would be deadly poison had a modified effect when rubbed upon the skin, and merely induced trances and visions.

I must be careful what I say upon the subject of these herbs, as I do not wish to encourage anyone who may be curious to dangerous and possibly fatal experiments. Suffice it to say, therefore, that a number of soporific and narcotic herbs grow wild in English woods and hedgerows. Wort-cunning, as it was called, has always been a part of witchcraft, not only for compounding magical salves and philtres, but to ease pain in the days when anaesthetics were unknown. Some of these herbs have also the property of making those who have taken a moderate dose of them more susceptible to hypnosis.

Hypnotism, too, is something that has been known as a magical secret from the earliest times, and is nowadays being rediscovered. It is evident from the fantastic stories told in all seriousness at witch trials, by people who claimed they had been turned into animals for instance, that witches could cast hypnotic illusions. If an old-time stage hypnotist could make one of his subjects run about on all fours and bark like a dog, to the delight of the pit and gallery, why could not a witch do the same?

The compendium of the laws of England compiled by Britton in the thirteenth century condemns the practice of "enchantment, as those who send people to sleep". This power was not always used in a malicious way. I have heard of witches who delivered women from the pains of childbirth by making them look steadily at the bright blade of a sword. It was not until the 1840's that Dr. James Braid, one of the pioneers of medical hypnosis, rediscovered the method of inducing the hypnotic state by making his patients gaze steadily at a bright object.

A well-known dislike of fishermen, in Sussex and elsewhere, is to meet a woman on the shore when they are setting off to fish. The reason, of course, is that the woman might be a witch. Witches were supposed to be able to control the winds by the sympathetic magic of whistling for them. The fisherman's real fear was that the woman might whistle up an unlucky wind. This is also the origin of the old saying:

> *"A whistling woman and a crowing hen*
> *Are neither good for God nor men."*

I am told that there are rules for whistling for the wind. One must consider the season of the year, and the wind that is most natural at that season. You must also consider the weather on the day you make the attempt. For instance, if the weather is warm for the time of year then you are not likely to find it easy to raise a wind of a cold nature, and would do better to try another. In general, the most likely wind to call in winter is the east wind. In spring the north wind is the wind of the season; in summer, the south wind; and in autumn the west wind. The east wind is cold and dry, the north wind cold and wet, the south wind warm and dry, and the west wind warm and wet.

Having considered these points, you turn in the direction of your chosen wind and give a long piercing whistle, three times. I am told that the best time to do this is at sunrise, and that farmers used to try to "*call the wind*" like this if their fields had been too much wetted by rain.

It will be remembered that all the cases of prosecutions for witchcraft in Sussex tried at Horsham and East Grinstead Assizes were for injuring people or animals, and some-times for killing by witchcraft. It was believed that some witches were able to injure simply by gazing fixedly at a parson or an animal. Such people were said to have the Evil Eye. Their witchcraft was known as "*eye biting*" or "*overlooking*".

Other methods of injury were to make a wax or clay image of the victim, and pierce it with pins or roast it slowly over a fire. An animal's heart stuck with pins and put up a chimney to dry in the smoke was also used to bewitch a person. In this case the pins were sometimes stuck in to form with their heads the pattern of the person's initials. Or an onion stuck with pins, and with a scrap of paper bearing the ill-wished person's name attached to it, was put up the chimney in the same way.

These methods of bewitchment were very much feared, and various counter-charms were practised to combat them. One of them was to draw blood from the suspected witch. In 1593 a woman called Elizabeth Drinkwater of Rye, Sussex, believed that a certain Mother Rogers had bewitched her child. She went to Hastings to consult with a white witch or *cunning man*, called Zacharias. He advised her to fetch blood from Mother Rogers by sticking a knife into her buttock. Elizabeth, however, thought this advice rather too drastic, so she compromised by pricking Mother Rogers in the hand. The child recovered, and of course this was attributed to the counter-charm.

In about 1561 a woman called Mother Margery was expelled from the town of Rye for practising black witchcraft. She was believed to have worked upon one victim until he hanged himself. She lived in the almshouses, and when her home was searched some pieces of raw beef were found. The entry about her in the archives of Rye does not say how she used them, stating only that her offences were *'such as any Christian harte wold abhore to here spoken of much less to be used.'* Probably they were used in the same way as the animal's heart mentioned above, namely stuck with pins and hung in the chimney.

The heart stuck with pins could also be used as a counter-charm. If someone's sheep or pigs died, and it was suspected that they died by witchcraft, the practice was to open the body of one of them, take out its heart, and stick it full of pins. Then it was either hung up the chimney or thrown on the fire. It was believed that this would cause the witch either to come to the house to beg forgiveness, or to die herself. So long as the smoke-dried heart remained in the chimney, no witch would have power over the animals of that household; but to burn the heart on the fire was sometimes thought to have a more drastic effect on the witch herself. The burning was accompanied by an incantation, while the fire was sprinkled with salt:

> *"It's not this heart I wish to burn.*
> *But the person's heart I wish to turn,*
> *Wishing them neither rest nor peace*
> *Till they are dead and gone."*

This sounds suspiciously like an incantation which could work either for defence or attack.

Has the belief that one person can influence another by the power of thought any foundation in reality?

F. T. Elworthy, in his book *The Evil Eye*, published in 1895, tells the following remarkable story from Somerset, where he lived. A farmer's boy left his employment against the wish of his master, because he wanted to better himself. He took a job at another farm nearby. Soon afterwards, he was seized with a terrible pain in his foot, so that he could neither stand nor drive home the cows. An acquaintance coming by found him in this state, and took him home in his cart. He advised him to consult a white witch or *"cunning man"*, as they were often called. The boy went to the cunning man who was known locally as "Conjurer __". He was told that somebody was working harm upon him. The cunning man advised him to return to his former employment, and to keep a sharp watch on the farmer and his wife to see if they took anything out of the chimney. " ..'n if they do," said the 'cunning man', "and tear un abroad, they can't never hurt thee no more."

The boy took his advice. His former employers asked him many questions, but eventually they took him back into the house again. He kept watch, and one day shortly afterwards he saw the farmer's wife take an image down from the chimney. He saw that the feet of the little figure, or "mommet" as he called it, were stuck full of pins and thorns. He made sure that the witch-wife had destroyed it, and then he ran off again back to the job he preferred! His feet had got well directly, and he knew that she could not harm him a second time. Elworthy adds that the names of all the parties to this story were known to him, and "Conjurer ____" occupied a cottage belonging to his father.

It was widely believed that some Sussex witches had the power to stop horses and carts so that they could not move. The witch who lived on Ditchling Common was credited with this power. So also was another witch who lived in a thatched cottage, now demolished, between the Half Moon and Plumpton. Carters were reluctant to pass close to their dwellings.

They also avoided if possible a cottage by the Sussex Pad, near Old Shoreham Bridge. This was the residence of yet another witch who practised the cart-stopping trick.

There were alleged counter-charms to this trick. One was for the carter to cut notches on the spokes of the bewitched cart's wheels with a knife. For every notch the witch was supposed to get a cut upon her fingers. Another was to run the blade of his knife around the iron tyres of his wheels. This was both a cure and a preventative, when in a dangerous neighbourhood. He thought if anyone was in the act of bewitching him this would cause them to cry out in agony.

If there is any foundation in fact for this legendary power of stopping a horse-drawn cart by witchcraft, then it must surely have been the horses, and not the carts, that were affected. Horse-lovers often assert that their horses see things invisible to humans, and will refuse to pass some apparently harmless place.

Inquisitors and witch-hunters declared that witches possessed familiars, which were demons or imps in the form of small animals. The witch was supposed to feed these imps by suckling them. In popular belief, one of the Devil's marks which he bestowed upon his devotees took the form of extra nipples. Alternatively, the imps were said to demand a spot of the witch's blood for every service they did.

Actually, a witch's familiar was a normal pet which was kept to make use of its psychic perceptions. Divinations would be made by observing its behaviour. It is a very old belief that animals can see and perceive what humans cannot. Nowadays, the Parapsychology Laboratory at Duke University, U. S. A. has been investigating extra-sensory perception in animals for some years. It has collected hundreds of cases, many of which involve premonitions of approaching danger.

Cats and toads are traditional witches' familiars. Toads actually make quite feasible pets so long as they have some water. They live on insects, and were kept in old-fashioned gardens for this reason, to destroy the pests.

The origin of the belief that familiars were suckled or fed was, in my opinion, a certain ritual action. Witches would give their familiars a spot of their blood in order to form a psychic link between the familiar and themselves. If the witch was a nursing mother, she would give a drop of her milk.

Gipsy horse-tamers had a traditional practice akin to this. They made a cake of oatmeal, honey, and lucerne, and carried it next to their skin so that it absorbed some of their perspiration. They kept the horse fasting for a day and a night, and then gave him the cake to eat and turned him loose. They claimed that after he had eaten the cake he would not only follow the man who gave it, but would seek him out and find him among a crowd. Every time the horse came thus to his master, the man would spit in his mouth and anoint the horse's tongue with the spittle. Treated thus, the horse would never forsake his master. There would be such a bond between them that the horse would even be able to divine his master's inner thoughts and wishes.

There is an obvious likeness between this practice and the belief behind it, and the practices and beliefs associated with witches' familiars.

A Sussex witch was supposed to be unable to die until he or she had passed on the powers they possessed to someone else. This shows the surviving memory of a traditional cult, whose members passed on secret knowledge from one generation to another.

Sussex Witch Beliefs

The traditional meeting-place of Sussex witches is Chanctonbury Ring. This is a high crest of the Downs crowned with a clump of beech trees which form a well-known landmark. They cover the site of what was once a Romano-British temple. A circular bank and ditch forms the actual Ring.

Tradition says that if you go to the Ring at midnight, run three times round it, and invoke the Devil, he will appear. Alternatively, it is said that you must go there in the dark of the moon and walk seven times round the Ring when the Devil will come out of the wood and offer you a bowl of soup. This latter tradition sounds like a memory of the days when feasts were held there on the Great Sabbats.

The traditions about coven meetings on Chanctonbury Ring date back to long before the time when local archaeologists found the remains of the pagan temple there. This shows how traditions about the witch cult do in fact link up with the old paganism.

Some other examples of this may be quoted. For instance the Rollright Stones in the Cotswolds are another pagan sacred place which is a traditional meeting-place of witches. Local people believe, though they are reluctant to discuss it, that witch meetings take place there periodically to this day.

The same tradition attaches to the Hoar Stones in Pendle Forest, Lancashire, and to the Bambury Stone on Bredon Hill, near Tewkesbury.

Another such group of stones is the Stiperstones, in Shropshire. Among them is a seat-like rock called the Devil's Chair. Here the Devil, or his human representative, is said to have presided over meetings of the Shropshire witches. Tradition says that if anyone else sits in the Devil's Chair a storm will arise.

A strange tradition attaches to Ditchling Beacon, the highest point of the Downs, 813 feet above sea-level. This height also is crowned by an ancient earthwork. For centuries it has been haunted by a phantom hunt, known locally as the Witch Hounds. Listeners hear the cry of hounds, the hoof-beats of galloping horses, and the call of the hunting horn, but nothing is seen.

This, of course is another version of the legend of the Wild Hunt, which is found all over Europe. In Windsor Forest its leader is Herne, a phantom rider crowned with the antlers of a stag, whom Lewis Spence in his Minor Traditions of British Mythology considers to be a form of Cernunnos.

A weird relic of Sussex witch beliefs found its way into an auction sale at Stevens' Rooms, King Street, Covent Garden, in January 1935. It was a mummified human hand, with the thumb missing. The auctioneers' catalogue stated that it was the hand of Mary Holt, who was hanged for witchcraft at Pulborough in Sussex *"nearly 200 years ago"*. It was said to have been used in the eighteenth century *"to cure all diseases"*. The missing thumb was said to have been cut off for a previous crime.

Now, no witch would have in fact been hanged as late as the 1730's. The last recorded hanging of a witch in England was that of Alice Molland at Exeter in 1684. Nor would the punishment of cutting off a thumb have been legal in the 1730s.

However, there is a tradition that a witch called Jenny lived at or near River Common, Pulborough. Also, there was a witch called Mary Holt, but she was an Essex woman. She was tried at Chelmsford in 1618 for bewitching two women and causing the death of one of them, and found guilty. Her ultimate fate is unknown, but such a verdict at that time and place may well have resulted in a hanging.

Perhaps this story may be disentangled thus: the mummified hand of Mary Holt, who was hanged for a witch in 1618, came into the possession of the witch Jenny of Pulborough two hundred years or more ago, and she used it as a magical relic to perform cures. Then somehow it found its way into the auction rooms in 1935, with a garbled version of its history attached to it.

After brisk bidding, the hand was bought for £3.15s., and vanished again from history. But how did Jenny get hold of it, if she did get hold of it? And how did it find its way into a London auction? And who bought it? And where is it now?

I doubt if it was used to cure all diseases; but there is a very old belief that a goitre or swelling in the neck can be cured by having it touched three times with a dead person's hand. In the old days when there were public executions, sufferers used to be taken to the gallows where the hanged felon's body was exposed. The hangman would be paid a small fee for the use of the corpse's hand. If my theory is correct, this is the way in which Jenny probably used the mummified hand; and Mary Holt was still performing witchcraft more than a hundred years after her death and for all I know may be doing so still!

Building repairs and renovations carried out on old Sussex houses often yield curious finds. For instance, an old bottle full of bent pins sometimes comes to light. It was a custom to bury such a bottle under the hearthstone, as a charm to prevent the occupants of the house being molested by witches. During some alterations to an old cottage at Heathfield, a cow's horn carved round the base with the signs of the zodiac was found. This probably had some magical use.

Along the window-sills of old cottages were placed the quaint little fossils known as "*Shepherds' Crowns*", to protect the house from lightning. These are actually fossilised sea-urchins found in the chalk. They are of two kinds, one loaf-shaped and one heart-shaped; but both have a marking upon them which resembles a five-pointed star. This is probably what caused them to be regarded as magical objects. They have been so regarded from very primitive times. The same Shepherds' Crowns beloved by Sussex cottagers have been found as grave-goods in Stone Age burial places, notably in a grave in the Neolithic camp on Whitehawk Down, near Brighton. They might even be the "*Serpents' Eggs*" or magical "*Glane-Stones*" of the Druids, that Pliny wrote about.

A person finding one when digging or ploughing was supposed to pick it up, spit on it, and then throw it over the left shoulder. If this little ceremony was omitted, bad luck would follow. In other words, the Shepherds' Crown was a powerful magical object which had to be treated with respect.

Some old cottages would display on their window-sills a regular little shrine of Shepherds' Crowns, holed flints and horseshoes, neatly and symmetrically arranged. This was to protect the inhabitants from lightning, witchcraft and the Evil Eye.

The flint stone with a natural hole through it was known as a *"Witch Stone"*. Sometimes one or several of these would be hung up at the house door as a protection against witchcraft. Sometimes one would be attached to the key of the stable to protect the animals from the *"eye-biting witch"*. I have seen one large holed flint which, from its smoked appearance, had evidently been hung up a chimney. The chimney and the hearth-stone, being as they were the warm centre of the household, were favourite places for concealing charms to avert witchcraft and the Evil Eye from the family circle.

It was evidently the holed shape of the Witch Stone that gave it its magical properties, as in later years round iron washers were hung up on houses and stables for the same purpose. It probably originated as a female sex symbol.

Like the Shepherds' Crown, the Witch Stone is of great antiquity as a magical object. Naturally perforated pebbles were found with Romano-British urn burials on Lancing Down, Sussex. If I am right in thinking that they derive their power and magic from being female sex symbols, then they may have been buried thus as symbols of the portal of rebirth or reincarnation. Shells, another female sex symbol, are often found in primitive burials, I believe for the same reason.

Also called Witch Stones are the small fossil sponges (Porosphaera globularis) with a natural hole through the middle which makes them look like white beads. These are found in the chalk and among the shingle on beaches. A good place to look for them is on Brighton beach between Black Rock and Ovingdean. People wore them round their necks for luck. Sometimes necklaces were made of them for the same purpose, with the "beads" neatly graduated in size. Sometimes Brighton fisher-folk would hang one of them on a piece of coloured thread or ribbon by their fireplace.

You can tell a real Witch Stone of this type from an ordinary white holed beach pebble by its roundness and neat shape, and by looking carefully at its surface, if necessary with a magnifying glass. Though perfectly smooth, it will display the characteristic porous appearance of a fossil sponge.

Certain magical markings are sometimes found on ancient cooking utensils. These are often called *"Witches' Marks"*, that is, charms to ward off witchcraft and evil spirits. One of the molestations of witches was to turn milk sour and spoil food. Mr. H. F. Fitt, writing in Vol. 9 of Sussex Notes and Queries (1942-1943), describes three such vessels which he acquired in Sussex.

One was a skillet bearing the name *"John Kempe"* on the handle, and the date *"1716"*. This was decorated with a pentagram, or five-pointed star, and *"a crossed pair of V's"*. The other two were a handled mortar and a three legged cooking cauldron of earlier date. These bore a mark *"rather like an amateur attempt at an enlarged pentacle"* (pentagram). All these marks were in relief, and therefore must have been made in the mould in which the vessel was cast.

I mentioned this matter to Mr. N. E. S. Norris, of the Barbican House Museum, Lewes. He showed me a picture of a Romano-British food vessel of the third or fourth century A. D., which he himself had dug up from a hut floor in Findon Close, West Blatchington, Sussex. This vessel bore a figure of a pentagram, which had been scratched on after the pot was baked, by the user. It says something for the continuity of tradition in Sussex that an identical pre-Christian *"Witch Mark"* should have been in use upon food vessels from Romano-British times to the eighteenth century.

The pentagram, or Star of Solomon, as it is sometimes called, is a very old magical sign. Mediaeval magicians used it to command spirits. It should not be confused with the hexagram, or Shield of David, the symbol of the Jewish religion. This is a six-pointed star, which was, however, also used in magic.

Rudyard Kipling, the well-known author, knew a white witch in Sussex, an old man called Bruffy Bostock. (Country people apply the term *"witch"* equally to man or woman.) Old Bruffy was the only man Kipling had ever met who could transplant any tree from one place to another with the certainty that it would grow and thrive. Kipling declared that in his opinion this was pure magic, and worked because the old man was one with nature, and his powers were the result of ancestral intuition. He may have been right, as in Cheshire in the early eighteenth century there was a famous white witch called Bridget Bostock, who possessed remarkable healing powers. She may have been Old Bruffy's ancestress.

People around Burwash came to Old Bruffy to have their warts charmed. They had to write on a slip of paper how many warts they had, and where they were. He would give them an ointment to apply, and the warts would fade away. But to make the cure work he had to be told the number and place of the warts. Proof that the power resided in Old Bruffy and not in the home-made ointment lies in the story that one village girl gave him a list specifying a number of warts on her hand, but was too modest to tell him the location of one upon her body. She duly received some ointment, and applied it to all the warts, but only the ones upon her hand disappeared. The other wart stubbornly remained until she had specifically asked for it to be charmed away.

Another male Sussex witch was Old Adullam who lived in the nineteenth century near West Hoathly, in what is still known as Adullam's Cave in the Valley of the Rocks. He evidently had no fear of the phantom black hound who is believed to haunt this valley. He himself is said to have been much dreaded by some of the local people.

Yet another male witch was a man named Braysher of Hurstpierpoint. He was famed for his skill in healing, but when offended he could put spells on both men and animals. He was credited with the power to bewitch a team of horses *"so that they couldn't move nohows"*.

Another Hurstpierpoint witch who could do the same was a lady locally known as *"Dame Prettylegs"*. Her real name was Mrs. Still, and she was the wife of a well-known smuggler. She also specialised in the Tanglefoot Charm, which caused people to wander out of their way and be unable to find their destination. One wonders if her husband ever got her to work this upon the Preventive Officers!

A witch in the Chailey district is said to have punished her maid with the Tanglefoot Charm if they were disobedient. When the maid went out for a walk, the witch would put the charm on her, so that she wandered out of her way and got lost. When she finally found her way home, the witch would mockingly reproach her for lateness.

In the year 1830, so Charles MacKay tells us, the town of Hastings had two residents who were firmly believed to be witches. One of these was an old lady who lived in the Rope-Walk. She was bent double, and walked with a crutch. She wore a red cloak, and possessed unusually bright and malignant eyes. She looked "*the very beau ideal of a witch*". It was believed, too, that she could assume the form of a cat when she chose.

Far from resenting the popular opinion of her, she encouraged and delighted in it. She would curse freely anyone who offended her. Her neighbours were terrified of her.

The same town's other uncanny resident was a fisherman, who was said to have a compact with the Devil. He was believed to have initiated his daughter into witchcraft too. "*He could creep through a keyhole*", they said; in other words, go about as a "*fetch*". It was also believed that he could sit on sharp points and feel no pain. The other fishermen used to put this latter story to the test. When he went to drink in an alehouse, they used sometimes to hide long needles in the cushion of the chair he sat in. Apparently, he never felt them. This was taken as confirmation that he must be a witch; a relic, perhaps, of the old practice of "*pricking*".

Probably he was cunning enough to realise what was said of him; and he exploited the test to increase belief in his powers, by the simple stratagem of a pair of well-padded breeches.

Folk Rites

Rituals connected with the Old Religion became a part of the life of country folk, sometimes when their real origin had been more or less forgotten. Such rituals were usually connected in some way with fertility.

Such, for instance, is the ceremony of worsling the apple trees. *"Worsling"* is the Sussex version of wassailing, from the Old Norse *wes heill*, *"be in health"*. This rite was observed in Sussex during the old Twelve Days of Christmas, and often on Christmas Eve. Those taking part were called the *"worslers"*, or the *"howling boys"*.

They would go to the chosen apple orchard at night, and stand in a circle round a tree, or a group of trees, depending how many worslers were taking part. Then they would rap the trees with their sticks, and sing a traditional song. This version of the song was taken down at Chailey many years ago:

> *"Stand fast, root,*
> *Bear well, top.*
> *Pray the God send us*
> *A good howling crop.*
> *Every twig, apples big,*
> *Every bough, apples enow.*
> *Hats full, caps full,*
> *Full quarters, sacks full!"*

Then they all shouted "Hurrah!" in chorus, at the top of their voices. To add to the din, one of the worslers blew loudly upon a trumpet made from a cow's or bullock's horn.

This apparently was an essential part of the ceremony. They went from tree to tree, or from group to group, until they had "worsled" the whole orchard. Then they would return to the owner's house and recuperate their voices with a traditional wassail bowl of ale, sugar, nutmeg and roasted apples. This drink was known as *"Lamb's Wool"*.

It is notable that this old song, which I have set down exactly as it was recorded, invokes not *"God"* but *"the God"*. It may be merely a dialect variation, of course; but it sounds rather like an invocation to a particular god of fertility. Also, just any trumpet would not do for the ceremony; it had to be one made of an animal's horn. This provides yet another link with the old Horned God.

I do not say, of course, that this ancient deity was always deliberately and consciously invoked; but that such rituals have their origin in the invocation of the old gods of fertility. Christina Hole, in her book English Folklore, has noted a lingering belief among country folk in beneficent powers which were other than Christian, and which were vaguely designated as *"Th' old Providence"*.

One such providential personage is the traditional *"Old Woman"* who starts the spring in Sussex by letting the cuckoos out at Heffle Cuckoo Fair every year on April 14th. *"Heffle"* is Heathfield on the map and about the middle of April is, of course, when the cuckoo usually arrives. The story goes that a mysterious *"Old Woman"* releases the cuckoos from her apron on that day and sends them to go cuckooing through Sussex woods and waken the spring. We may see in this *"Old Woman"* the figure of an ancient goddess of Nature.

The cuckoo in ancient times was a sacred bird of the Mother Goddess, and appears as such in figurines and carvings from Crete and Mycenae. The sceptre carried by Hera was surmounted by a cuckoo. The meaning probably was that it was she who brought the spring.

In old belief, all cuckoos were female. The cuckoo's mate was the wryneck a small bird of the woodpecker family who gets his name from his way of twisting his neck round when surprised. His old name is the *"Jynx"*. He was thought to be a magical bird, and was used in spells. It is from this circumstance that the word *"jinx"* comes, meaning a bringer of bewitchment.

Perhaps from its connection with the old Nature-goddess, the cuckoo is a bird of divination. It is said that whatever you are doing when you first hear the cuckoo in spring is a presage of what you will be doing for the rest of the year. Hence it is fortunate to hear the cuckoo first when you are out walking in the woods. This is a sign that you will have a pleasant active year, especially if its cry comes from the right.

From the left it is not so fortunate, and may be a warning. It is unlucky to hear the cuckoo first when you are lying in bed, as this means danger of illness for yourself or your family. When you hear the cuckoo for the first time, you should turn your money over, to ensure plenty in the year ahead. You may also make a wish, and if it is a reasonable one it is sure to be fulfilled.

Another bird of divination is the magpie. The old rhyme about them says:

"One for sorrow, two for mirth,
Three for a wedding, four for a birth,
Five for silver, six for gold,
Seven for a secret that's never been told."

To see one magpie on the left-hand side of you is specially unlucky; but the misfortune may be averted by taking off your hat and bowing to the bird.

These beliefs relate directly to the old pagan practices of taking omens from the behaviour of birds and animals. They too believed that omens on the left were unfortunate. In fact, our word *"sinister"* literally means *"on the left-hand side"*.

A particular day for fertility rituals in Sussex was Good Friday. This is probably because it coincided with the old festival of spring. The Brighton fisher-folk used to take part in skipping games on that day. Both grown-ups and children used to join in, all skipping together over one long rope. This practice seems to be akin to the leaping dances performed as sympathetic magic to make the crops grow tall.

At Hove, the young men and girls used every Good Friday to visit a certain mound, the burial place of some ancient chieftain. They danced around it and on it, and played kissing games. George Aitchison, in his Unknown Brighton, says:

"The right to kiss and be kissed on this hill on Good Friday was
as unchallengeable as the right to kiss and be kissed under the
mistletoe on Christmas Day."
- George Aitchison

Both this and the kiss under the mistletoe derive from ancient fertility rites that originally went far beyond kissing.

In 1857 this tumulus was levelled and built on. Inside it were found human bones and grave-goods, including a beautiful amber cup, now a treasure of Brighton Museum.

One of the pagan practices prohibited in the Laws of King Edgar, A. D. 963, and under King Canute in A. D. 1018, was the making of offerings to wells and fountains. Nevertheless, this was a very widespread practice, down to modern times. The people of olden time considered the sources of pure water to be sacred, and inhabited by spirits. The Moon-goddess was the ruler of water. One of the derivations of here name Artemis is *"High source of water"*.

Robert Charles Hope, in his book The Legendary Lore of the Holy Wells of England (London 1893), quotes a Saxon homily against witchcraft and magic which says:

> *"Some men are so blind that they bring their offerings to immovable rocks, and also to trees, and to wells, as witches teach."*

He also states:

> *"The particular times when it was considered most propitious to visit the wells, appear anciently to have been at daybreak or sunrise in May and at the summer solstice."*
>
> - R C Hope

These, of course, were festivals of the Old Religion. Later, the Christian Church rededicated the wells to saints, and changed The Times of visiting them to Easter and Ascension Day. However, the old pagan beliefs still showed through their Christian disguise. There was actually (and may still be) a sacred well near Witton, Yorkshire, dedicated to *"Saint Diana"*!

There was a wishing-well at Buxted, in Sussex, and *"holy wells"* at Eastbourne, Horsted Keynes and Steyning. Perhaps the most celebrated Sussex well was the Pin Well at Lewes. Pin Wells are so called fro the old custom of dropping pins in them and making a wish. In the old days, pins were more costly articles than they are today, and were a favourite from of offering to sacred wells.

The Pin Well at Lewes was a spring that burst out from the chalk ridge and flowed into a neighbouring brook. It was within the grounds formerly belonging to the Priory, and was approached by steps. When Hope wrote of it in 1890 it had been covered over; but its site was marked by a stone tablet with *"Pin Well"* cut on it. Pinwell Road on the map of Lewes still gives us a hint of its location.

With regard to sacred stones, Sussex does not possess any surviving stone circles. There are a number of traditions, however, showing that it once possessed them. For instance, the great stones heaped around the base of the fountain in the Old Steine, Brighton, once lay in Goldstone Bottom, and were believed to be the remains of *"Druidical temples or altars"*. (History of Brighthemlston, J. A. Effedge, 1862.)

In the Valley of the Rocks at West Hoathly is a strange stone group known as Big-on-Little, or Great-upon-Little. An old man once told the folklore collector J. P. Emslie (1839-1913) of a tradition attached to this rock. People said that it had formerly been an object of worship, and *"to touch it was death"*.

The group consists of a gigantic rock poised upon a smaller one. This again stands upon another large rock; so that the whole group resembles a titanic human head, neck and shoulders, rising out of the earth. Its locality is believed to be haunted and uncanny. Not far away is the cave chosen by Old Adullam the witch for his residence.

The village of Rottingdean possesses a curious ritual observance connected with a strange carved stone let into a flint wall nearly opposite the church. This is known locally as *"The Wishing Face"*. It is a crude representation of a goblin-like face, evidently much older than the wall in which it is set. Underneath it, marked in its cement setting, is the date *"1306"*. The story goes that if one makes a wish while rubbing the nose of the figure, the wish will come true. From this belief the nose has acquired a fine polish. I have not been able to find the origin of this belief, or of the stone.

Sussex possesses one of the most remarkable relics of ancient belief to be found in Britain. This is the famous figure of the Long Man of Wilmington, cut into the turf on the side of Windover Hill, looking down on the truly beautiful little village of Wilmington.

Many famous antiquarians have speculated as to the age and meaning of this figure; but it looks through the summer haze on the green hillside as mysteriously as ever.

During the nineteenth century it had been allowed to fade to *"a mere phantom-like appearance, to be seen only when the dew or hoar frost were on the turf"*. So a newspaper described it in 1874. In that year, however, the Sussex Archaeological Society, to which the figure now belongs, had it restored and outlined with white bricks, and has since continued to preserve it.

Sir Flinders Petrie gives its measurements as being 226½ feet in heath for the figure of the *"Man"* himself, and 230 feet and 235 feet respectively for the two staves which be holds in his outstretched arms. The figure is designed skilfully to counteract the effect of foreshortening when seen from below.

The Long Man's obvious analogy is the famous Giant of Cerne Abbas, in Dorset. This latter figure is a magnificent, virile piece of work, not only outlined but modelled in relief. In one outstretched hand he bears a club, and the features of the face and the nude body are plainly indicated, unlike the Long Man, whose body is a mere discreet outline. I have heard of a tradition, however, that the Long Man was once as ithyphallic as his brother at Cerne; but that in the Middle Ages the monks of Wilmington Priory went up Windover Hill and obliterated that feature of the Long Man which they found objectionable.

There is no doubt of the Cerne Giant's connection with the cult of fertility. J. S. Udall, F. S. A. , in his Dorsetshire Folklore, tells us that it is said to be a certain cure for barrenness in women if they sit on the figure of the Cerne Giant; though some say the man and woman desiring a child must actually have sexual intercourse on the figure. A former Vicar of Cerne put a stop to the festivities attending the *"scouring"* or cleaning of the Giant, which was done about every seven years, *"as they tended to practical illustration of the above superstitions, which did not conduce, it was thought, to the morality of his parishioners"*.

Another version of the belief mentioned above is that the woman desiring a child must spend a night sleeping in the open air upon the Giant. Dylan Thomas wrote one of his finest poems, In the White Giant's Thigh, upon this tradition.

The Cerne Giant was connected with the old fertility rituals of May Eve, one of the witches' Sabbats. In former times the Maypole was erected every year on the hill just above the Giant, and the accompanying festivities were such as to arouse the ire of the righteous. A Puritan writer, Philip Stubbes, in his *"Anatomie of Abuses"*, published in 1583, described how in his day hundreds of people spent the night of May Eve in *"pastimes"* in the woods and groves, returning in the morning with green branches and garlands to deck the maypole:

> *".. this 'stinking idol' rather, and then fall they to banquet and feast, to leap and dance about it, as the heathen people did, at the dedication of their idols, whereof this is a perfect pattern, or rather the thing itself."*
>
> -P Stubbes

Puritan Stubbes evidently realised quite well that the maypole was a phallic symbol, and the modern version of the huge emblem of Priapus which was similarly decked and danced around before the coming of Christianity. We have seen how the Sussex maypole used to be topped with the witch's besom.

At night, the Beltane bonfires blazed, and there was more leaping, feasting, dancing, and probably more *"pastimes"*. I have heard it credibly reported, (Stubbes continues) and that viva voce by men of great gravity and reputation, that of forty, three score, or a hundred maids going to the wood over night, there have scarcely the third part returned home again undefiled.

In Sussex the heights of the South Downs made fine bonfire sites, and they are remembered as taking place on Firle Beacon and Mount Caburn, not far from Wilmington. If these festivities took place in connection with the Cerne Giant on May Eve, it is reasonable to suggest that they also took place in the vicinity of the Wilmington Giant, and that both figures represent the old god of fertility.

In 1924 the Bexhill Museum Association paid a visit to the Long Man of Wilmington and Mr. Henry Kidner, F. G. S., read a paper to them in which he said:

> *"The custom was in early times at the beginning of May, to gather in its (the Long Man's) vicinity and to make merry with excessive indulgency in the firm belief that such practices would have a magical effect upon nature, and would promote the growth of vegetation - Such annual celebrations took place at Cerne Abbas, until not many years ago a clergyman had them suppressed."*
>
> - H Kidner FGS

There is another stray scrap of tradition about Wilmington. It says that if you go to Wilmington Crossroads at midnight and take with you a black cockerel, the first person you meet there will be the Devil or his representative, and he will be able to grant you a wish.

In the old days Wilmington Crossroads may well have been the rendezvous for those who intended to make their way up the hill on ritual nights.

ⓦ

Ⓦhite Ⓦitchcraft

Ⓘn this chapter I will try to give a small collection of folk remedies and magical practices which deserve to be classed under the above heading.

Firstly, some methods of charming warts. One of the oldest beliefs is in the medicinal virtue of *"fasting spittle"*; that is, the human saliva first thing in the morning, before anything has been taken to eat or drink. If this is gently stroked on to a wart or a sore each morning, it is believed that it will eventually cure it. Mothers have also used this method to charm away babies' birthmarks.

The finger to apply it with is the ring finger of the left hand. This finger was anciently called the leech finger, *"leech"* meaning a doctor. Its touch was supposed to have a magical healing quality.

A charm that I know to have been practised with success in my own family is to rub the warts with the downy inside part of a broad bean pod, and then bury the pod. As it decays, so the warts will vanish.

Another old charm to remove warts, which again connects up with moon-lore, was this: when the moon is at the full, go outside into the moonlight with an empty basin. Dip your hands into the basin, and make a pretence of washing the affected part, while looking up at the moon. Repeat three times as you do so, *"I wash the warts away"*.

A charm to cure small burns was to repeat the following, while pointing with the leech finger at the burn:

> *"Here come I to cure a burnt sore.*
> *If the dead knew what the living endure*
> *This burnt sore would burn no more."*

Then the charmer had to blow a cooling breath three times upon the sore place.

Another curious charm for healing burns or inflamed places has a definite connection with the old belief in the triple Moon-goddess.

68

Three bramble leaves washed in spring water were used. The following charm was said three times over each leaf as it was laid on the sore:

> *"There came three ladies out of the east.*
> *One brought fire and two brought frost.*
> *Out fire and in frost!"*

The leaves were then bound on to the sore place.

A Christianised version of this charm makes the *"three ladies"* into *"three angels"*, and adds the words *"In the name of the Father, Son and Holy Ghost"*. However, the former pagan version is evidently the older.

Sometimes the words of healing charms were kept secret. They were muttered inaudibly, usually three or nine times, over the injured place. Sometimes the place would be gently stroked or held, depending on the nature of the injury. When the words were a secret, they could only be rightly taught by a man to a woman, or by a woman to a man. Otherwise they would have no virtue.

In any case, the patient had to come to the charmer in complete trust and confidence of a cure. The charmer must be neither thanked nor paid, though they could be given a present after the charm had worked. The following is one such charm to cure a sprain:

> *"These words were writ on a marble stone,*
> *Flesh to flesh and bone to bone,*
> *Sinew to sinew, vein to vein,*
> *And each one to its rest again."*

A small piece of elder wood with three, five or seven knots in it, cut from a tree growing in a churchyard, and worn close to the skin, was an amulet against rheumatism.

An amulet and a talisman are not the same thing. An object which is an amulet is solely to avert some evil. A talisman, on the other hand, works actively to procure some particular benefit of luck or love.

Plants or trees figuring in herbal spells are often specified as *"growing in a churchyard"*. It will be remembered that our older churches were deliberately built upon places already sacred to paganism. So the churchyard in an old village stood a good chance of having been a pagan sacred place. This is what gave the plants and trees in it their magical virtue.

The Sussex shepherds who spent much of their time upon the open Downs had often to brave the dangers of thunderstorms. They had a rhyme which contains sound advice in these circumstances:

> *"Beware of the oak,*
> *It draws the stroke.*
> *Avoid the ash,*
> *It courts the flash.*
> *Creep under the thorn,*
> *It can save you from harm."*

In addition they often carried in their pockets a *"thunderbolt"*, as an amulet against the lightning. This was a lump of iron pyrites, a natural crystalline form of sulphate of iron found in the chalk.

Sussex shepherds had a way of counting their sheep which was considered to be *"proper"* and fortunate. This was to use, not the usual numbers, but certain traditional words. Here is the count up to thirteen:

"Yan, Tan, Tethera, Pethera, Pimp, Sethera. Lethera, Hovera, Dovera, Dik, Yan-a-Dik, Tan-a-Dik, Tethera-Dik."

These numerals are among the oldest utterances of our language, being survivals of the old Celtic speech before the Angle-Saxon Conquest.

A piece of sympathetic magic worked by Sussex women who desired an increase in their family was to rock an empty cradle. There is an old rhyme about this:

> *"If you rock the cradle empty,*
> *Then you shall have babies plenty."*

Perhaps the most famous talisman of fertility, wealth and love is the mandrake. It is mentioned in the Bible (Genesis, Chapter XXX). The childless Rachel, Jacob's wife, begged his other wife, her sister Leah, for the mandrakes that Leah's son, Reuben, had found growing in the fields. Leah made a bargain with Rachel that she should have the mandrakes on condition that she made Jacob spend that night with

Leah instead of her. Rachel evidently believed so ardently in the magical virtue of the mandrake that she agreed; and the bargain was worth it, as afterwards Rachel gave birth to a son, Joseph.

In the Middle Ages many strange legends grew up about the mandrake, and were fostered by those who wanted to keep the secrets of the plant to themselves. It was said to shine in the dark with an unholy light. It was said to be engendered beneath the gibbet upon which a man had been hanged. It was said to utter such a fearful shriek when plucked from the ground that anyone hearing it would be stricken with madness and possibly death.

The story was told that the only way to pluck it up was to tie a hungry dog to the plant by his tail, and then show him some meat. The dog would leap at the meat, and in 10 doing would pull the mandrake from the ground, and himself fall dead. Then the mandrake gatherer, who had taken the precaution of stopping his ears with wax, could take up the plant in safety.

All this, of course, served to keep up the price of mandrakes as powerful and rare talismans. I have heard today of a high price being asked for a good specimen.

Now, the mandrake which grows in the Near East and the warm Mediterranean countries is the Atropa Mandragora. Apart from its magical virtues, it yields a narcotic drug. It is quite true that the root is very large in proportion to the rest of the plant, and that it bears a curious resemblance to the nude human form, sometimes male and sometimes female. In this resemblance the magical virtue lies.

However, the Atropa Mandragora in Britain, according to the old herbalists Gerarde and Parkinson, was only to be found nursed up as a rarity in herbalists' gardens. It would not be available to the country witches. Nevertheless, Francis Bacon in his Natural History tells us of :

> "... mandrakes, whereof witches and impostors make an ugly image, giving it the form of a face at the top of the root."
> - F Bacon

The plant they used was the English Mandrake or White Briony (Bryonia Dioica). This is a climbing plant which usually grows in hedges.

Says the old herbalist Culpeper:

"The root groweth to be exceeding great, with many long twines or branches going from it, of a pale whitish colour on the outside, and more white within."

- N Culpeper 1616-1654

This root by witches' art was made into a fantastic image, which was the talisman. I have seen a huge female mandrake, most skilfully carved, and with the representation of a child in either arm. Its owner firmly refused to part with it. It appeared to be very old.

This is the way in which the mandrake talisman is made. First, a good mandrake plant must be found. Then, on the night of the full moon, you must dig a hole on either side of the hedge in which it is growing. This will enable you to work slowly towards the root, using a small digging tool and a pair of cutters to snip through the intervening roots of brambles and thorns. When you get to the mandrake root itself, work with your bare hands to avoid damaging it. You will need to dig thus all round the root to loosen it, as a really large mandrake needs considerable effort to pull it from the ground. It will actually make a groaning noise as it is drawn from the earth.

The root must be pruned of straggling parts, leaving the *"arms"* and *"legs"* of its human shape. Then a *"face"* is carved on it. Sometimes small roots are left in the appropriate place for *"hair"*, and the human appearance is perfected according to the skill of the carver. The root is then reburied in a safe place until the next full moon, when it is dug up again. By this time the pruning and carving will have healed over, so that it appears to have grown naturally in human form.

The mandrake must now be dried slowly and carefully over a fire until all traces of moisture are gone. The fire must be sprinkled now and then with the magical herb vervain (Verbena officinalis), to bathe the mandrake in its sweet smoke. If the root is very large, it may take several months before the drying operation is complete. Then it is dedicated to occult use, and kept carefully wrapped in clean white linen.

Women used to bear small mandrakes hung about their waists under their skirts, as a charm to make them sexually attractive and fertile. Men carried them close to their skin to enhance their virility. The big mandrakes were kept in the house as a general charm for fertility and prosperity.

There is one particular time of the year when the moon forces are at their most powerful. This is at midnight of the first full moon after the winter solstice. This was the time chosen by witches to dig the mandrake root or to cut a forked hazel twig to use as a divining rod.

Divining, or *"dowsing"*, for water is still done in Sussex. It is said that the best results are obtained if the operator goes barefoot, and walks slowly in a north and south line. The forked part of the rod is held in the hands, palms upwards. I once helped someone to divine for water, and can testify that the rod is pulled strongly downwards as one passes over certain spots. I was surprised at the strength of the movement. This method was also wed to search for metals and for buried treasure.

The St. John's Wort (Hypericum perforatum) was believed to have magical properties if gathered on Midsummer Eve, the Eve of St. John. A bunch of it hung on the wall of a bedroom dispersed evil hauntings and brought pleasant dreams to those who slept there. Like all herbs gathered at this time, its efficacy was increased if it was held over the smoke of a ritual Beltane bonfire.

Another powerful charm worked on Midsummer Eve was the making of the *"Lucky Hand"*. This talisman was made from a root of male fern (Dryopteris filixmas). The root was dug, and the curled fronds cut away until only five were left, so that the trimmed root resembled a hand with five hooked fingers. The Lucky Hand was then smoked over the bonfire, and preserved as a charm to bring good luck to its possessor, and to defend him against ill-wishers and evil spirits.

Old-time herbalists were often asked for a piece of the scarlet gum-resin called dragon's-blood. This was for the purpose of working a love-charm. The gum had to be pounded in a mortar to break it up. Then some of it had to be wrapped in a piece of paper on which the beloved person's name was written. This had to be secretly burned on the fire, on a Friday night, as this incantation was repeated:

> *"It's not this herb I mean to burn,*
> *It is ___'s heart to turn.*
> *May he no peace nor comfort find*
> *Till he comes to me and speaks his mind."*

Then the operator of the charm had to retire to bed without speaking to anyone. The charm had to be repeated for three successive Friday nights.

Friday has been from time immemorial the day ruled by Venus, according to magical lore. The Sun ruled Sunday, the Moon Monday, Mars Tuesday, Mercury Wednesday, Jupiter Thursday, and Saturn Saturday.

Up to comparatively recent years, old-fashioned herbalists also used to sell the roots of tormentil (Potentilla tormentilla) for working a love-charm. This was secretly made use of by many a lovelorn housemaid, and perhaps, if the truth were known, by their mistresses too.

The root had first to be ground up, or pounded small in a mortar. Then, when the opportunity arose, a pinch of the root was secretly dropped into the tea-pot in which tea was being made for the desired person. The worker of the spell had to stir the pot three times, and whisper into it:

> *"Tormentil, Tormentil, make _____ subject to my will."*

Then, if the person named drank the tea with them, the spell was cast. This is actually a piece of sympathetic magic. Tormentil, according to old herbals, is an astringent or *"binding"* herb. So those who partook of it in this way would be bound together.

A white witch's talisman to attract love to the woman who wore it was a little bag of herbs which had been picked at the full moon and carefully dried. This was pinned inside the clothes, next to the skin. Its contents were usually the all-potent vervain, and southernwood (Artemisia abrotanum). This latter plant gained its country name of *"Lad's-Love"* from the belief in it as a love-charm. It will be noted that it is one of the Artemisias, which take their name from the Moon-goddess. A piece of orris root (Iris florentina) might be added for its fragrance.

A grim talisman in which, nevertheless, Sussex people put much faith was a fragment of wood cut from the gibbet on which a man had been hanged. A favourite luck-bringer in the Ditchling area was a fragment from the gibbet on Ditchling Common on which a pedlar was hanged for murder in 1734.

A highly valued possession in old times was a crystal ball for crystal-gazing or scrying as it was called. These would be kept very secretly, and sometimes handed down in a family for several generations. A genuine crystal ball is a valuable object, more so than one of glass. Antique shops in the Brighton Lanes sometimes display crystal balls for sale, often at high prices. They are usually not crystal at all, but merely glass, though they may be genuinely old. They should have a little stand of turned or carved wood.

I am told that the great difference between crystal and glass is that friction or warmth, as when the globe is held in the hands, excites electricity in pure crystals, whereas there is no such power in glass. A good test of a pure crystal is its icy coldness when held against the cheek, more so than a glass ball. Also, I am told that a crystal ball is much heavier than a glass ball of the same size.

Psychic researchers have collected many cases of clairvoyant visions obtained by "*scrying*". Some have advanced the theory that gazing into the crystal produces a mild state of auto-hypnosis, in which the unconscious mind is free to extend its perceptions and bring them to the surface of consciousness. Many instruments have been used to bring this state about, such as glass balls, "*magic mirror*", or even a bowl of water; but all scryers agree that a genuine crystal has a special quality.

It is said that the best time to attempt crystal-gazing is at twilight or after dark. The one who makes the attempt should sit in a darkened room with their back to the light, which should be a dim lamp or a candle. They should wash their hands before taking up the crystal. Then they should sit calmly and passively with closed eyes, holding the crystal in their hands until it becomes warm. After sitting like this for about five minutes, the "*power*" will have accumulated in the crystal.

Then it should be replaced on its stand and gazed steadily into, from about as far off as one would a book one was reading. Look into the centre of the crystal, not on the surface. One should not continue longer than about ten minutes at first. Eventually, if one has the faculty, some symbol or vision will be seen.

The crystal should never be washed, but polished with a wash-leather and kept in a wash-leather bag. Nor should it ever be exposed to bright sunlight; but the rays of the moon are good for it.

Some old-time scryers believed that it helped their powers to drink a tea made of mugwort (Artemisia vulgaris), before attempting to practise the art Mugwort has from the earliest times had a reputation as a "*witches' herb*". Its Latin name tells one reason why. It was sacred to Artemis, the Moon-Goddess. Having tasted it, I can testify that mugwort tea is quite harmless and not unpleasant. The herb should, of course, be gathered at the full moon to be of greatest efficacy.

There is a definite connection in old belief between crystal-gazing and the moon. If the crystal is exposed to moonlight, it makes it more sensitive. The art is best practised when the moon is waxing. The scryers' potion is made from the herb of the Moon-Goddess. The belief in the potency of the crystal may really be based on the fact that crystal is one of the semi-precious stones "*ruled*" by the moon.

Mugwort, like vervain and St. John's Wort, was one of the magical herbs of protection to be gathered on Midsummer Eve, and hung up in the house to preserve it from black witchcraft and evil spirits.

Another instrument used by witches for scrying is the magic mirror. Although more rarely seen than the crystal, nevertheless specimens do occasionally come to light in the shops of antique dealers. Instead of being backed with a reflecting substance, like an ordinary mirror, the magic mirror is black. It is usually mounted in a wooden frame, carved with magical sigils. Some mirrors are convex, others concave, and others flat. The best specimens are said to be the concave mirrors.

Traditionally, the best substance with which to back a speculum of this kind is turpentine asphaltum, or Stockholm tar, the black residue which is left after the turpentine has been distilled. In the days of the old sailing ships, this substance was used on the ships' timbers. Hence it would have been easily obtainable in coastal towns. A poor witch who could not hope to won a crystal ball would make herself a magic mirror, which would serve the same purpose.

Having obtained a suitable piece of glass, the witch had to coat the back of it with three coats of turpentine asphaltum. After each coat was applied, the mirror had to be "*magnetised*" by holding the hands over it and making passes over it, clockwise with the right hand and anti-clockwise with the left. Of course, each coat had to be dry before the next one was applied. Then the glass was enclosed in a suitable wooden frame.

This work was best undertaken in the waxing moon. On a night of the full moon the mirror had to be *"consecrated"*, to dedicate it to magical use.

The rules for developing clairvoyance with this instrument were similar to those for the use of a crystal. The scryer had to sit regularly in a darkened room, holding the mirror in both hands. Results usually commenced by the mirror assuming a cloudy appearance. When this cleared away, visions would commence to appear.

When not in use, such a mirror would be kept carefully hidden, and wrapped in a black cloth.

Finally, to show how strong and deep are the roots of ancient belief in Sussex, let me quote this story which was told in the Sussex Notes and Queries, August 1944. A Mr. Frank R. Williams wrote of what he called *"a lingering survival of paganism"*. He had witnessed it near South Harting in 1924.

He was watching an old ploughman just starting his day's work, and he saw him drop into his first furrow a scrap of food. It was a portion of the packet of food he had brought with him to work. Mr. Williams asked him why he did this. All the old man could tell him was that it *"brought luck to the land"* - A sacrifice to Mother Earth in the twentieth century!

Present Day Witchcraft

Since the last of the Witchcraft Acts were repealed in 1951, it has become something of a popular gimmick to proclaim oneself a witch.

Such claims have frequently been made on radio and television and in the popular Press. I have personally met many people who claim to be "*witches*" or members of "*witch covens*".

My experience is that the louder and more frequently such claims are made, the less likely they are to be genuine. Real witchcraft, which certainly still exists, is a secret thing. The very last thing a possessor of real secrets does is to seek cheap publicity.

Hence, authentic information about present-day witchcraft is hard to come by. So also, for obvious reasons, is such information about the practices known as black magic. This latter term is sometimes wrongly used to describe almost any occult ritual. There are instances, however, in which its use is justified. Anyone who claims that black magic does not exist is either simply ignorant of the facts, or is trying to conceal the truth for his own ends.

Magic and witchcraft, both black and white, live on in the modern world, and are believed in. Nor is it only the primitive and the uneducated who put faith in them.

I feel sure, from what I have been told, and such scraps of information as have come my way, that Sussex is not the only county where witchcraft is still practised. For instance, there is an active cult of white witchcraft in the West Country. Its members call themselves the White Ladies, and specialise in healing. Nor are they the only witchcraft group in the West Country and the Cotswolds.

I have heard of covens in Lancashire and Yorkshire; in the Epping Forest area; in Surrey; and in the New Forest in Hampshire. Traditions of witchcraft still survive strongly in lonely parts of Essex and of course in Scotland. I have also heard of witch meetings in

Northamptonshire in recent times. I have been told of ancient rituals carried on in the Channel Islands and in Wales.

However, it is apparent that the old traditions survive in fragments. Possibly no one coven today possesses them all. The years of persecution have taken their toll; but it is still possible for the serious student of folklore to attempt to gather up the fragments again and piece them together to make a complete whole.

His efforts may be confused at first by the foolish activities of publicity-seeking poseurs. However, experience will enable him to sort out the genuine from the bogus. The writer would like to make it clear that she herself is merely a student, setting down the results of her researches and recording, with their permission, what has been told her by others.

The following is a brief outline of the basic beliefs of the Old Religion of witchcraft. Firstly, witches believe that the physical world is only a part of reality; that part which happens to be perceptible to our physical senses. There are many subtle forces, they claim, which are not generally known or recognised.

They believe in a supreme Divine power which is the original source of all things. Out of this Ancient Providence come the gods and goddesses, and the hierarchies of spirits in their many orders.

The divinities of the witches, the "*Old Ones*" are the primordial gods. They are the personifications of the forces of Life, Death and Resurrection. They are nameless, having countless names. They are primitive, shared with all nature. For this reason they have been depicted in animal as well as human forms. They have been pictured by mankind in various ways, in different ages and places. Such mental images have a real existence on planes more subtle than the physical. Their details symbolise the powers they represent. Consequently, they enable mankind to forge a link with those powers by means of his imagination.

Symbolism is the language of the unconscious, the language of dreams. It can awaken echoes in deep, primitive levels of the mind. Carl Gustav Jung, the psychologist, probing these deeps of the mind, has rediscovered the ancient gods; only be calls them "*the archetypes of the collective unconscious*".

The particular patron gods of the witch cult are those whom the Thessalian witches of old images as Pan and Hecate. The horns of Pan are the primordial symbol of power. The horned phallic god of fertility is also the god of death and the world of spirits. Like Janus, he is the opener of the gate of death and the gate of life. The power of fertility is Life itself, continually being resurrected from death.

The Moon goddess in her three forms, the crescent moon, the full moon and the dark waning moon, is perhaps the most ancient deity conceived by man. She is the seducing mistress of magic, the archetypal witch.

She is also the moon mother, enabling all things to come to birth. Primitive man saw her every lunar month disappear into the dark Underworld and reappear again, bringing the moisture which is the life of all growing things. He saw that she ruled the tides of the sea, and also the mysterious tides of fertility and barrenness in women, by her twenty-eight day recurrence. The ancients planted their crops, and worked their magic, according to the phases of the moon.

The Moon-Goddess and the Horned God are still the deities witches worship and invoke. Worship and invocation are the means by which the mental image of a divinity is ensouled and comes to life.

Another basic belief of the witch cult is in reincarnation. This belief was very widespread in pre-Christian times, and was accepted by some of the early Christians. However, it was condemned as a heresy by the Church Council of Constantinople in A. D. 553.

After this condemnation, the belief ceased to be taught openly m the western world. However it retained a firm place in folk traditions. For instance, the people of the West Country in Britain firmly believed that King Arthur would come again.

Between incarnations, the dead are thought of as dwelling in the Land of Faerie, a pleasant country rather like that of earth, but without its sorrows and ugliness. Some times they are able to revisit the earth and talk to mortals. There is even one case on record of a Scottish witch Bessie Dunlop of Dalry, Ayrshire, whose familiar spirit was one Thom Reid, who had died at the Battle of Pinkie in 1547. Bessie Dunlop was tried and executed for witchcraft in 1576. By means of Thom Reid's assistance she had been able to help the sick and find things lost. Her acquaintance with him lasted some four years, during which time he furnished her with convincing proofs of his identity.

He told Bessie that he had been asked to help her by the local "*Queen of Fairies*"; that is, the chief woman witch of the district. That this lady herself was no spirit is shown by the record of her visiting Bessie. She is described as a stout woman who sat on a bench and drank beer with her!

It was after this visit that Thom Reid started to appear, the facts of this case were recorded by Sir Walter Scott in his Letters on Demonology and Witchcraft, years before the ideas of modern Spiritualism were ever heard of.

Not all inhabitants of Faerie, however, are discarnate humans. Witches believe that we are by no means the only intelligent beings to inhabit the universe. On the contrary, they say, there exist many orders of beings in nature which never have been, nor will be, human; but which, nevertheless have their place in the scheme of things. Such spirits are not in themselves either "*good*" or "*evil*". They are just "*different*". These, too, can sometimes attach themselves to humans as familiars.

In witchcraft there are said to be three degrees of initiation. A witch tradition frequently encountered is that knowledge must be passed from one sex to another; that is from a man to a woman or from a woman to a man. Exceptions, however, are made of the witches' own children. There are a number of records, for instance, of a mother initiating her daughter.

Many details of witch initiations have survived, and can be collated into an intelligible whole. The new initiates must take an oath of secrecy. They are given a new name, as the indication that they have assumed a new magical personality. Their initiator makes them kneel, and places one hand upon their head, the other beneath the sole of their foot. In this position, all between the hands is dedicated to the witch cult and the witch faith.

They are shown the ritual "*working tools*" of a witch, and their use is explained. Probably they are given or lent some already consecrated things, as it is necessary to have consecrated objects in order to make a new set for oneself. This is the magical link down through the ages.

As initiations usually take place at a Sabbat or Esbat, the newly made witch takes part in the ritual meal with the rest of the coven. There is a very old belief that if people eat and drink together it creates a psychic bond between them. One sees traces of this attitude in those primitive tribes who will never attack a stranger once he has shared their meal. It survives also among civilised people, who will pointedly refuse to eat or drink with someone who has offended them.

The old Sabbats and Esbats are still kept up. As we have seen, there are four Great Sabbats, namely Hallowe'en, Candlemas, May Eve, and Lammas. There are also four Lesser Sabbats, the Spring Equinox, the Summer Solstice, the Autumn Equinox, and the Winter Solstice.

These eight Sabbats make the Wheel of the Year, which turns at Yule, the season of the Winter Solstice. The word "*Yule*" means "*the Wheel*". For centuries before Christianity, the death and rebirth of the sun was celebrated at Yule. Eight is a number of fertility, because it is two, the male and the female, multiplied by itself and by itself again.

There are thirteen lunar months in a year, and hence thirteen full moon Esbats. This may be the reason why witches revere the number thirteen. Thirteen is regarded as the ideal number to form a coven; though in these days a district may not be able to muster a full coven of thirteen.

Traditionally, the meeting-place of a coven must be at least a league (three miles) from the meeting-place of any other coven, to avoid clashes of interest. Also it is the tradition that anyone coven shall not know too much about others. Only the senior members keep in necessary contact with other covens. Then, in case of any trouble arising, what people do not know they cannot reveal.

There is no doubt that these very ancient ritual practices have a profound psychological effect on those who take part in them. For one thing, they seem to arouse latent psychic powers and perceptions.

I have been given an eye-witness account of how a party of people climbed a height of the Sussex Downs one night at the full moon, to contact the ancient powers. Their purpose was partly to carry on a tradition, and partly to feel, if only for a moment, that kinship with the forces of life which is the deep root of primitive religion.

They carried with them an old ritual knife, known as an Athamé, which would be upheld in the hand of their leader as the invocation was pronounced. They also had a plate of metal engraved with a five-pointed star. This is the pentagram, the symbol before which evil spirits are daunted and abashed. Such a plate itself, engraved with magic signs, is called a pentacle.

The materials for a small fire were taken, and a flask of wine, together with a large old-fashioned drinking-cup made of horn. Both the knife and the cup were inscribed with magical sigils.

It was a fine night of bright moonlight, with a strong wind, and a few flying clouds passing across the moon. My informant described the climb up the hill, and how they reached the summit already in a state of suppressed excitement. They lit their fire, choosing a slight dip in the ground so that it would not be visible to any watching eye in the village below.

Then the leader took up his position before the fire, with his back to the wind so that the flames were blown away before him. In his right hand he bore the ritual knife, in his left the pentacle. The others stood in a semicircle behind him. A woman bore the horn cup filled with wine.

An old man had been given the task of tending the fire, so that it should neither die out nor flare high enough to be seen from afar. He crouched at one side of it, with a stock of dry wood. My informant was told that wood for the fire had been collected the previous day, and hidden nearby.

For a few moments all stood in silence, then the leader gave a peculiar, long-drawn-out call, something like:

"*EEE-OOO AAH-YOH-AIEE!*"

A thrill passed through the little group, and some of them instinctively linked hands.

The leader began to recite an invocation. It called upon "*the Old Ones*", and the powers of the elements, earth, fire, air and water, to bless "*this time and this place and they who are with us*".

The woman with the cup of wine went up to him. He held the knife high, so that the gleams of moonlight and firelight shone on the blade.

Then he lowered it into the cup held out to him. The symbolism of the act was obvious. As the knife was male, so the cup was female. From union proceeded blessedness and fertility.

The woman who bore the cup drank a little from it, and then gave it to the leader. As she did so, she took the ritual knife from him, and held it while he drank. Then the cup was passed from hand to hand, and all drank from it. The little that was left over the woman poured upon the ground.

Beside the fire the leader laid down the pentacle. Upon it the woman placed the empty cup. The leader set down the ritual knife with its point inside the cup. The old man who had tended the fire drew from under his coal an old-fashioned musical instrument, something like a recorder. He began to play upon it a slow, tilting melody. Then all the rest joined hands and began to dance in rime to the music. They circled deosil (i.e. sun-wise, turning to the right) about the embers of the fire and the little symbolic group of ritual objects.

How long they danced my informant could not say. He told me that his senses were bemused by the moonlight, the wild night wind, and the scent of the fire. He felt that in this remote place he had taken part in a ritual which in its essence was as old as time.

Presently the music stopped, and the dancers came to a halt. The leader held up his arms, and gave the strange call again. There was a silent pause. Then he said, *"Merry meet, merry part"*.

The ritual objects were gathered up, and the embers of the fire made safe. The little party set off again down the hill. The companion who had brought him saw him on his way home. He was not encouraged to talk to the others present. They had met at a prearranged rendezvous, and been introduced by first names only. To this day he is not certain of their identity, nor, curiously enough, of their exact number.

He believes that taking part in this ritual had a definite psychological effect upon him. He describes it as *"a heightened awareness of the unseen forces behind the visible world of nature"*.

For some time afterwards he had a number of vivid dreams. Usually these took the form of flying effortlessly through wild, moonlit country. Sometimes he was accompanied, in his dream, sometimes alone. Once he distinctly heard in the course of a dream the old man playing his pipe; he found himself dancing with shadowy companions In the midst of a circle of stones. He found this series of dreams "*weird but definitely enjoyable*".

Another witch meeting was described to me as having taken place in an old house in an historic East Sussex town. This one was held on Christmas Eve. To outsiders it would have passed as just another Christmas party. Its purpose was to enquire into the future by means of "*scrying*" in a crystal ball. The seer was an elderly man. About half a dozen other people attended. They met in a large room in the upper part of the house, warmed by an open fire of logs. The windows were covered with thick curtains, to baffle prying eyes. Over the mantelpiece was a large pair of stag's antlers. Underneath them was an old wood-carving, blackened with age. It showed a male face with curling fronds of leaves and flowers coming from out of its mouth. This is the well-known figure of the "Green Man", a mediaeval version of the old Fertility-god of the woods.

The furniture and rugs had been set back to the walls, except for a small table and a chair in the centre of the room. Upon the table, concealed under a black cloth, was a crystal ball on a stand. Beside the crystal were an old ritual knife, a censer and a box of incense, and two pentacles. One was the five-pointed star. The other, made of white wax, was engraved with magical sigils. There was also a little hand-written book of sigils and invocations, a metal bowl of water, and a bunch of herbs.

Around the chair and table, as widely as the room would permit, a circle was drawn in white chalk upon the wooden floor. At the four cardinal points, just outside the chalk line, stood lighted candles in tall sticks, these and the firelight provided the only illumination.

The door was bolted, and the ritual commenced. Those present ranged themselves around the table. The seer said words of consecration over the water in the bowl, that it might purify the place of evil influences. Then taking the bunch of magical herbs, he used it to sprinkle the water around the circle.

Holding the ritual knife, he invoked the great beings who ruled the elemental powers to guard the four cardinal points. Throwing grains of incense upon the glowing charcoal in the censer, he carried it deosil about the circle. The room became filled with perfume and faint blue haze. The incense appeared to be ordinary church incense mixed with dried herbs.

Then the seer held his hands over the crystal, and invoked the "Old Ones" to send true visions, by means of the spirits whose sigils were engraved on the wax pentacle. He seated himself at the table, and uncovered the crystal. My informant noted that he took care to sit with his back to the north. The others stood around with hands linked, and kept complete silence.

Several minutes elapsed, with the seer warming the crystal in his hands, his eyes closed. Then he gently replaced it on its stand, and fixed his eyes upon it. After a while he began to describe a scene which appeared to him, and said it applied to one of the people present. A woman he described was recognised by this person as a relative. He proceeded to make a number of predictions relating to family matters which were carefully listened to.

Another of those present was told about the affairs of his son then serving with the Forces overseas. A woman was told of a journey she would take in the coming year; another about a man she was friendly with. Various predictions were made about local and national events. The seer spoke in a quiet, even voice, as if in a dream. The listeners remained still and silent, hanging on his words.

Nearly an hour had elapsed when the seer's voice fell silent. He uttered a deep sigh, and seemed to come out of a light trance. Looking round, he indicated that this was all the spirits were revealing at that time. The séance was at an end.

He stood up, and expressed thanks to the spiritual beings for their assistance. Then he cast more incense upon the glowing embers in the censer, and carried it again around the circle. Finally, he took up the little bunch of herbs, and again sprinkled drops of the consecrated water about the room. This was to dismiss any lingering unseen entities that the ritual might have attracted.

The assembly adjourned to the sitting-room below. Everyone relaxed and joined in a Christmas drink: "*To the Old Ones! Merry meet, merry part*".

My informant was told that the seer's visions were remarkably accurate. However, he would only sit for members of the coven. To outsiders, he would deny having any knowledge of clairvoyance, or even any interest in such subjects.

He had inherited the crystal ball and the little hand written book from his grandparents. His parents had preserved the legacy, but had taken no interest in it. Upon his father's death it had come to him, and he had begun to study the old traditions and develop the gift.

Two members of this coven were a young farmer and his wife. They told my informant that at one time their crops had not been doing well. They asked the leaders of the coven if they could help. The coven held a ceremony at which they consecrated a talisman. This was to be buried deep in the defective field in the waxing moon.

The leaders told the young couple to choose a fine night on which to bury the talisman. They were to do so secretly, telling no one, and letting no one see them. When the talisman was buried, they were "*to lie together upon the earth and perform the rite of marriage*".

They followed these instructions. Afterwards, they said, they had the best crop they had ever had from that field.

Another ceremony that was described to me concerned the evocation of elementals. This ritual was performed on the night of a midsummer full moon, by the seashore. The spot chosen was a lonely one, where the participants were unlikely to be disturbed.

Those taking part included the old man who had played the recorder for the Esbat dance on the hilltop, and a young woman who was to dance to his music. Her dance would invoke the Moon-goddess who rules the sea to permit the spirits of the sea to manifest. Another man was to act as seer.

The little group foregathered on the shore, and found a clear patch of sand. The tide was low, but coming in. The moon made a glittering pathway on the water. They did not light a fire this time, for fear of attracting attention from fishermen or others who might be within sight of the shore. Instead, they had brought a large censer to burn incense. They drew a large circle upon the sand with the Athamé and stood within in it. Outside the circle, pointing towards the sea, a triangle had been drawn. Within the triangle was drawn the sigil of the elemental spirits of water.

The charcoal within the censer was kindled, and incense cast upon it. As it burned, a cloud of perfumed smoke mingled with the scent of the sea. The censer was carried by one of those present. Another held the pentacles. One inscribed with sigils of the powers of the moon.

The girl who was to dance stood with her hair loose and her feet bare. Around her neck was an old necklace of silver, set with moonstones.

The circle was consecrated and fortified by invoking the guardian spirits at the four cardinal points. An invocation asking for the blessing of the "*Old Ones*" and the aid of the Moon-goddess was spoken. The elementals of the sea were called upon to appear.

Then the old man, standing in the centre of the circle, began to play upon his pipe. Although quite untrained, he possessed considerable musical skill. His plaintive, improvised melody seemed to harmonise perfectly with the night, the moon and the sea.

The girl began a graceful, slow dance, deosil about the circle. The others stood in silence, watching the breaking waves.

The dancer had a natural grace, and a little professional training. Her barefoot dance, with now and then her arms upraised to the moon, in those surroundings was remarkably effective. A sense of timelessness seemed to come over the little group. The music, the rhythmic movements of the dancer as she circled them, the sound of the waves, were having an hypnotic effect.

Presently, the seer whispered to his companions that "*he could see them out on the waves*". The music slowed gradually to an end, and the dancer sank to her knees, arms upraised, facing the moon. The seer declared in a low voice that he could see a moving procession of shadowy forms passing over the tops of the waves. The forms, he said, were indistinct at first. As soon as he looked directly at one, it vanished, or melted into another. Presently they became clearer. They were like tall, graceful people, and seemed to be gay and laughing.

Then he said that, closer into the shore, among the waves as they broke upon the beach, he could see smaller forms, like merry, naked children dancing and playing. They were about a foot high, and he could hear the voices *"like silvery bell"*. The girl who had danced said she could see them too.

For some time they watched the play of the elemental spirits. Then clouds began to pass across the moon, and the incoming tide crept nearer. The forms became more indistinct to those who could see them. It was time to bring the ritual to a close.

The bearer of the pentacle with the five-pointed star carried it deosil around the circle, upholding it at the four quarters, east, south, west and north. The elementals were *"licensed to depart"*. The guardian spirits were hailed and thanked. Fresh incense was cast into the censer, and a last cloud of it was borne about the circle. Then the contents of the censer were cast into the approaching waves.

As the little party took its way from the beach, the sea covered the sigil upon the sand, the circle and the footprints. I was told that such ceremonies are not performed out of idle curiosity, but for a definite purpose. This purpose is to bring humans back into a living kinship with nature. Once a person has had even one of these experiences of contacting the forces behind the world of form" he or she is no longer in mental bondage to that world. Their own elemental vitality awakens, in kinship with the rest of nature.

I was reminded of Rudyard Kipling's friend, old Bruffy Bostock, who could do remarkable things because he was *"one with nature"*. Did he, too, know the People of the Elements, the Undines, the Dryads and the Fauns?

Modern Black Magic

remarked in the previous chapter that anyone who denied the present day existence of black magic was either simply ignorant of the fact or was trying to conceal the truth for his own ends.

A full qualification of that statement would almost require another book. However, some significant stories from the national Press may give the reader food for thought.

Not long ago three young businessmen took a flat together in Nottingham. The house in which the flat was situated had previously been empty for some time. The new tenants of the flat happened to go exploring in the basement. To their surprise, beneath the cellar they found another cellar.

Here, carefully painted upon the walls, were weird and fantastic figures. One was of a blood-stained hand. Others were of devils' heads. An upturned box, stained red, seemed to have been used as a kind of altar. It was caked with the dripping, of candles.

Rather shaken, one of them told the story to a reporter for a Nottingham newspaper. The reporter asked him if he thought it could have been done as a joke. He replied that he thought the drawings were too well done, and too much trouble had been taken with them, for that. Besides, surely a cellar beneath a cellar was an odd place to play jokes?

The paintings appeared to have been done recently. Had the arrival of the new tenants disturbed some person or persons who had been using the empty house for strange rituals?

I mention this story because, unknown to him, it bears a remarkable similarity to one told me by a Brighton man. He and another man once stayed overnight in a rented room in a tumbledown old house in Brighton. They were rather hard-up at the time, and glad to get a cheap lodging. However, one night in this particular place was enough for them.

They had to share the squalid room. They tried to sleep; but as the night wore on an increasing sense of fear and strangeness came over them. The room was invaded by a chillness which seemed something other than mere cold. Finally, the atmosphere of unearthly evil became so intense that they could stand it no longer. They got up and dressed, and resolved quietly to explore. Anything was better than remaining still in that weird place.

They crept downstairs to the kitchen. All was normal; there seemed no visible reason for their fear. Then, greatly daring, they decided to venture farther, to a cellar-like room below.

They looked in; and upon the bare floor they found the obvious remains of some occult ritual. There were what the man called "*queer chalked signs*" drawn on the floor, and the burned-down remains of black candles.

They returned to their room, and sat up with the light on to await the dawn. In the morning, they left as soon as they could.

The house in question had a disreputable clientele, mostly from the fringe of the underworld. I had an opportunity, when it became vacant, of entering it. Apart from its dinginess and squalor, it certainly had a most unpleasant atmosphere. I can only describe it as a feeling that one wall being watched by something vicious.

My informant who had some knowledge of the occult, firmly believed that a ritual must have been performed there shortly before he and his friend had their uncanny experience; and that some evil entity attracted by this ritual was the cause of their terror.

The Sunday Empire News, on November 1st, 1959, the day after Hallowe'en, reported that the mutilated bodies of two cats had been found at Newcastle upon Tyne. The area where they were found is one of derelict buildings, near a railway station.

An R. S. P. C. A. inspector is quoted as saying, "Whoever killed those poor cats must have had warped minds. The manner of the deaths suggested that whoever did it was carrying out a ritual of being daubed with blood. Such as would happen, I suppose, if a person was being initiated into a secret society".

A Newcastle police spokesman suggested that it was the work of a teenage gang. It may have been, of course. However, the date of the discovery, so close to Hallowe'en, is significant.

I have heard a first-hand account, from a young man in Brighton, of a black magic ceremony which involved the ritual use of the blood of a cat. This young man, incidentally, is a different person from my informant of the previous story.

He told me how, a few years before, he had been doing his National Service. He became friendly with another young National Serviceman, whose people kept a large public house in the country. His new friend asked him if he would like to spend their next short leave with him there.

A country pub sounded attractive, so he agreed. Everything seemed perfectly normal. The premises were large and well appointed. One large upstairs room, he was told, was reserved for private parties. During the night he got up and went down a few stairs to the toilet. He noticed that a party seemed to be in progress in the large room. Being on leave, he was not averse to a bit of fun; so instead of returning to his bedroom, he decided to peep round the door where the party was taking place, to see if it looked lively. Frankly, he said, he was hoping they'd invite him in for a drink. If, however, it seemed a formal affair, he intended to slip off again without them seeing him.

Being in slippers and dressing-gown he moved quietly. He opened the door of the room without being noticed, and looked round. He found that he had gate-crashed a very odd "party" indeed.

All the lights were turned out, and the room was lit only by candles. Standing round in the gloom were men and women wearing dark robes and masks. In the centre of the room was a kind of altar, with incense burning upon it. Through the incense smoke he could make out a weird figure standing behind the altar. It was that of a tall man, dressed in a black robe embroidered on the breast with cabalistic signs. The man's face and head were covered by a horned, goat-like mask.

Completely astonished, the young man just stood and stared. As he did so, someone spotted him. Quickly he was grabbed, pinioned, and pulled inside the room. There was a moment of confusion as the participants realised they had a spy among them. Then the goat-masked leader told him that, as he had come so far there was nothing for it but for him to join the black coven and take the oath.

Although he was in the Forces, he was just a teenager, and by now thoroughly scared. He realised that to make an outcry was useless. In spite of the robe and mask, he had recognised his friend's mother, the proprietress, among those present. So, with his arms firmly pinioned by two men, he submitted to the grotesque ritual.

He was brought to the altar, and made to take a frightening oath of loyalty and silence. A black cat was killed upon the altar as a ritual sacrifice, and his face and wrists were daubed with its blood. They gave him a cup of some dark wine to drink. It was strong, and evidently laced with a drug, as he says that after taking it his recollection of what followed is hazy and confused.

He awoke the next morning and found himself back in his bed. He could have believed the whole occurrence a fantastic dream, except for one thing. Upon his face and wrists were traces of dried blood.

He did not know what to do. He did not know if his friend knew about it or not. If not, he had no wish to tell him. Anyway, who would believe him? It was his word against that of a dozen or so people. They would simply say that he had gate-crashed a private party got helplessly drunk, and had to be put to bed.

In the end, he decided to say nothing. His leave was up anyway, and he had to return to his unit that morning. So he just packed his bag, and left as soon as he could. All he wanted to do was to get away. He had put the experience out of his mind, and never spoken of it to anyone.

There was a time when I dismissed stories of black magic, involving blood sacrifices and even whispers of human sacrifice, as nonsense dreamed up by journalists in the silly season, to sell their papers. I no longer do so.

An indisputable instance of black magic ritual involving human sacrifice occurred recently in America. A man from Puerto Rico, Juan Aponte, forty-six years old, worked on a chicken farm near Vineland. New Jersey. One day he was arrested on a minor charge, and confessed to a murder.

His victim was a thirteen-year-old boy, Roger Carlotto, who had then been missing for some time. Roger had been in the habit of visiting Aponte, who gave him cigarettes. Outwardly, Aponte was a normal, respectable citizen. Secretly, he was a student of black magic and voodoo, who performed regular rituals.

Some details of the magic Circle he used, painted on a piece of canvas, are given in the account of his preliminary trial. It is recognisable as the one depicted by Eliphas Levi as the Goetic Circle of Black Evocations and Pacts. The police found a quantity of literature upon black magic in his possession.

Aponte desired to regain the love of a former woman friend, who had left him. For this purpose, he wanted a human victim, as the supreme sacrifice to evil spirits.

Chapter XXII of the famous Grimoire, The Key of Solomon, is entitled: Concerning Sacrifices to the Spirits and How They Should be Made. It begins:

In many operations it is necessary to make some sort of sacrifice unto the Demons, and in various ways. Sometimes white animals are sacrificed to the good Spirits, and black to the evil. Such sacrifices consist of the blood and some times of the flesh.

They who sacrifice animals, of whatsoever kind they be, should select those which are virgin, as being more agreeable unto the Spirits, and rendering them more obedient.

When blood is to be sacrificed it should be drawn also from virgin quadrupeds or birds, but before offering the oblation, say:

May this Sacrifice which we find it proper to offer unto ye, noble and lofty Beings, be agreeable and pleasing u-to your desires; be ye ready to obey us, and ye shall receive greater ones.

Then perfume and sprinkle it according to the rules of Art.

Aponte confessed that he killed his victim by striking him a blow upon the back of the head and then strangling him with a cord. He buried the body under the dirt floor in his home. Seven months later, he dug up the body, cut off the head, and carefully dried it in a stove. Then he performed a hideous ritual with a lock of hair from the head of the woman he desired, placing it within the skull of the sacrifice.

Six psychiatrists gave evidence at the preliminary hearing in the Aponte case. Aponte was found to be sane and sent for trial, charged with murder. The Press cutting I have of the case is from the Sunday Pictorial, dated October 5th, 1958.

Black magic sometimes involves the desecration of churches and cemeteries. I have been told of two alleged instances in which churches in Sussex were desecrated by having black magic rituals performed in them by intruders in the night. Another allegation I have heard involved the use of a Sussex graveyard for a black magic ritual. The body of a cockerel was said to have been found lying in a pool of blood on an old flat tombstone, which had been used as an improvised altar.

I could get no proof of these allegations; but they are in keeping with black magic beliefs. The idea involved is that more power is given to a ritual if it is performed on consecrated ground.

On June 29th, 1958, the Sunday Pictorial reported a police raid by night on a disused graveyard on an island in Loch Lomond, Scotland. They had received reports that black magic rituals were being carried on there. They failed to catch anyone, but found clear evidence of its use for ritual. Two black candles and an ornamental dagger were found hidden beneath a gravestone. A black cloth had been draped over the iron railings of a tomb; and the remains of black candles were found on altar tombstones.

A man living nearby testified to having seen boats going to the island by night. He said that he had seen fires and lights there, and heard sounds of chanting and screaming.

A horrible scandal of graveyards desecrated for black magic broke out in Finland in the autumn of 1931. Portions of a number of human bodies were found in a well near Helsingfors. The police at first feared that they had to do with a case of mass-murder. However, their investigations and the medical evidence soon led them to abandon this theory. Instead, they began to suspect that in fact they were dealing with black magic.

Their suspicions led them to the caretaker of a municipal mortuary, a man named Saarenheimo. They began exhumations in the cemetery where bodies which had passed through Saarenheimo's mortuary had been interred.

They found that over forty of the bodies they exhumed had been mutilated in various ways.

Saarenheimo was arrested. The police searched his lodgings, and found literature on necromancy and black magic, together with some incriminating letters. One of the treatises on black magic was in English. Another book was described as "an old Swedish 'Black Bible'". This sounds like a Grimoire.

His neighbours told the police that mysterious meetings had been taking place at night at the mortuary for nearly two years past. It was believed that a black magic fraternity of considerable size was involved, possibly even on an international scale.

Saarenheimo, in custody, frequently spent his time chanting cabalistic words. Meanwhile, the police continued their grim work of investigation. Great public concern had been aroused, especially in those families who feared that their dead had been outraged. Many persons were interrogated, but no further arrests were made though it seemed evident that Saarenheimo was not alone in this horrible affair.

As a result of this case, the Church authorities made careful investigations at all parish mortuaries throughout Finland, to prevent any possibility of a recurrence of Saarenheimo's crimes.

The facts from which the above account is taken were published in The Times on October 7th, 9th and 14th, 1931.

As to the purpose of these desecrations, there are many recorded black magic rituals which require human blood, candles of human fat, or lamps fed with oil made from human fat. Human bones, human skin, and parts of bodies have been used in black magic spells. The Act of Parliament passed by James I against witchcraft in 1603 also included a special provision against those who robbed graveyards for the horrid needs of black magic.

I have myself seen, in a private magical collection in London, a mummified human phallus that had been carefully mounted on a stand for some magical purpose.

Another terrible story came from Spain in 1920, and was reported in The Times on September 27th of that year, under the heading: Human Vampires. A young girl who was minding sheep in the province of Estremadura had been found murdered. Her body had been drained of blood, and mutilated of several organs. At the time when this occurred the Madrid police were already investigating the similar death of a little boy. Both deaths were attributed to practisers of black magic.

The Times correspondent commented that in spite of several severe penalties recently imposed upon what he called "*witch doctors*", fanaticism and superstition still preyed upon the people of remote villages, and human blood had still its price.

So much for the glib dismissals of those who try to persuade us that black magic does not exist!

I know of a shop in Brighton which specialises in selling Oriental joss-sticks and incense. The proprietor told me that there was one type of incense which he refused to stock, namely that scented with musk. He had formerly kept it, he said, until he found out that it was being used in the rituals of black magic.

That well-known writer on black magic, the late Montague Summers, always insisted that there was a secret black magic centre in Brighton. It does not seem to be generally known that at one time Montague Summers lived in Brighton. He is well remembered by one of the staff of Brighton Reference Library, where he used to study.

I have myself recently purchased in Brighton a curious pair of old candlesticks, in the shape of horned devils' heads. They may be a relic of some old-time "*Hell-Fire Club*". These fantastic associations were denounced by a Royal Proclamation in 1721. Nevertheless, they continued to be heard of as late as 1828. Most of their members were more interested in drink and bawdiness than in the occult. Some, however, had an inner circle devoted to curious studies and ritual.

Brighton was a favourite resort for Regency "*bucks*", who could indulge themselves there even more freely than in London. A peculiar feature of its architecture is that it possesses a great many underground tunnels and passages in the older parts of the town. Some of these were possibly natural caves, improved upon by the fantastic taste of

Georgian and Regency builders. A persistent local tradition states that some of these tunnels have at times been used for secret meetings.

I have heard from two different sources of a strange group of people who used to meet regularly in a house not far from Brighton seafront. The room in which they gathered to perform their ritual was said to be entirely painted and hung with red.

A more usual colour scheme for a room set aside for magic is black. The walls, ceiling and floor are entirely painted or draped with black, which acts as a background for the appropriate magical symbols. Some builders working on an old house, in a Sussex village that must be nameless, recently found such a secret room. They were very puzzled by what they took to be someone's odd taste in decoration!

Some time ago, another secret room was found in a village not far from Brighton. Some workmen were doing alterations to an old house there, and had occasion to dig in the grounds. They found a circular underground room, exactly nine feet in diameter. This is the traditional dimension of a magic circle. I believe a tunnel connected it to the house.

In times past many people of all ranks in society practised the occult arts. This secret cell may well have been used for some such end by a previous occupant of the house. A candle to provide light, a brazier of hot coals to provide heat and to burn incense, and a ventilation shaft, would have been all that was necessary to make it ideal for the purpose. Alternatively, of course, it may have been a *"priest's hole"*, a relic of the days of religious persecution. But if so, why go to the trouble of making it an exact nine-foot circle?

A modern practitioner of strange arts who lived in Sussex was the late Rollo Ahmed. In 1954 he was living in an old house in Hastings. An upper room in the house was used as a magical temple. Here Ahmed used to receive visitors, attired in a hooded purple robe, his face covered by a black mask. He was of Egyptian extraction, white- haired, dark-skinned, and with a neat Vandyke beard.

People came to his candle-lit temple to obtain talismans. Sometimes they came to seek relief from the spells and curses they believed to have been laid upon them by other practitioners.

On Hallowe'en, 1954, Ahmed staged a ritual at which thirteen people were present. Its purpose was to release a young man from a black magic spell which had been cast on him two years previously. He invited two newspaper reporters, in order, he said, to prove to them that people in Britain were interested in black magic, (Sunday Pictorial, November 7th, 1954).

Ahmed was the author of a book upon black magic entitled The Black Art. The well-known author Dennis Wheatley wrote a preface to this book, in which he acknowledges his indebtedness to Rollo Ahmed for the background information which went into his famous occult thriller, The Devil Rides Out.

That famous and controversial figure, Aleister Crowley, who gloried in the title of "*The Beast 666*" (he even had it printed on his visiting-cards!), spent the last two years of his life at Hastings. He died there on December 1st, 1947, aged seventy-two. His remains were cremated at Brighton on December 5th, and the ashes sent to his disciples in America.

The ritual which took place at his cremation caused protests to Brighton Town Council. It consisted of his Hymn to Pan, and some extracts from The Book of the Law and his Gnostic Mass. These were read from the rostrum of the crematorium chapel, while a congregation, mainly of his followers and friends, gathered about his flower-covered coffin.

Present also, but in his official capacity, was Superintendent Robert Fabian, of Scotland Yard. He tells of this occasion in an article he wrote after his retirement in the Sunday Graphic, June 10th, 1956. He states that, observing the congregation, he was able to identify leading members of known black magic circles in London, and also in the neighbouring towns of Lewes and Shoreham. He also mentions this in his book London After Dark.

I have been told that these people were not Crowley's own followers, so presumably they came out of curiosity. Aleister Crowley believed himself to be "*The Logos of the Aeon of Horns*". This new age of the world his followers believe to have commenced in 1904, when Crowley wrote the manuscript of The Book Of the Law. According to him, this manuscript was dictated to him by a superhuman, discarnate intelligence. From it he took his basic teaching:

"Do What Thou Wilt Shall Be the Whole of the Law. Love is the Law. Love Under Will."

He died a firm believer both in The Book of the Law and in magic. In his pocket-book after his death was found a parchment talisman inscribed in the magical script called Enochian. It was consecrated *"for a great fortune"*. He was using it to find a new mistress!

There was a rumour in Brighton that some difficulty had been experienced in carrying out the cremation. It was alleged that certain members of the staff at the crematorium had been so affected by the pagan ritual in the chapel that they flatly refused to touch the coffin. Whether true or not, this is a story by which Crowley himself would have been delighted.

A man whose life was darkened by his association with Crowley lived for many years a voluntary exile in Sussex. He was Victor Neuberg, the poet, who hid himself in the village of Steyning, near Chanctonbury Ring.

When he was a young man, he had been a follower of Aleister Crowley. He worked with him in performing magical rituals, and became a valued assistant. He also helped Crowley to produce the series of magical writings known as The Equinox.

A beautiful young actress whose stage name was Ione de Forrest joined their circle. She was unhappily married and separated from her husband. Victor Neuberg fell passionately in love with her. Crowley resented their devotion to each other. He wanted Neuberg to be his disciple, to be devoted to him and him alone. He was all the more angered when he heard that Ione was obtaining a divorce, and that Neuberg intended to marry her.

In his book, Magick in Theory and Practice, Crowley boasts that he caused the death of a woman by magical means. He describes her as a *"vampire"* who was seducing his disciples. This woman was Ione de Forrest.

Crowley says that he went to the door of her home and there drew a certain sigil in the air with a magical weapon. Shortly afterwards she shot herself.

What Crowley also did involved Neuberg himself. Part of their magical practices was the invocation and dismissal of spiritual entities. A ritual had been planned which involved the invocation of the powers of Mars. Crowley was to conduct the ritual and Neuberg was to be the medium through which the power of Mars was to manifest.

The time came for the performance of the ritual. The place of working was arranged, with the circle, candles and incense appropriate to Mars. Crowley spoke the preliminary invocations. Neuberg was given a drug to make easier the control of his personality by the powers of Mars. He performed a ritual dance in which the god Mars was invoked to possess him.

The invocation was successful. Neuberg, for the time being, became a vehicle through which the cosmic power of destruction personified by the god Mars became manifest.

Then, at the end of the ritual, Crowley played Neuberg a cruel magical trick. He deliberately omitted the banishing ceremony by which Neuberg's normal personality should have been restored.

For seventy-two hours after the ritual, Neuberg struggled against the obsessing power which was swamping his mind. Eventually, he gained the struggle, and the influence wore off. But in the course of that seventy-two hours, he had quarrelled violently and brutally with Ione de Forrest, in a way which, according to his friends was quite foreign to his normal nature.

Ione de Forrest was a highly strung, sensitive woman, with suicidal tendencies. Also, she had just learned that she was going to have Neuberg's child. It was after this quarrel that she shot herself.

Neuberg was overwhelmed with grief. From his magical experience, he knew what Crowley had done, and why he had done it. He never forgave Crowley, or himself.

He broke completely with Crowley, and also abandoned his promising literary career. He left London, and settled down in a cottage in Steyning, where he lived in complete obscurity for many years. Although he married, the tragedy of Ione de Forrest was never erased from his mind.

Like most subjects, witchcraft and magic have their bright and their dark sides. In this book I have tried to write fairly and factually of both. The distinction between white and black magic, and between white and black witchcraft, should not be lost sight of.

It is the distinction of methods and of motives. White magic and white witchcraft seek to serve some good purpose. Black magic and black witchcraft seek to corrupt and degrade, to grab, dominate and exploit.

A favourite garb which the followers of the black side adopt is that of pseudo-religion. However, the enquirer into these matters will not be deceived if he ignores high-flown pretensions and looks at results.

Many of the self-styled *"High Priests"* and *"Adepts"* are merely silly exhibitionists. Some, however, are as vicious as they are stupid and nasty. What they are really adept at is deluding their followers, and especially their women followers, that they are being initiated into magical secrets, when they are in fact being degraded and exploited to satisfy the *"Adept's"* personal desires.

Apart from the question of white or black, the distinctions between the different streams of occult tradition in Europe need to be understood. I have already touched on this point in Chapter Three.

While there is much common ground, witchcraft is basically the pre-Christian *"Old Religion"*, the worship of the forces of life and fertility, and the knowledge and use of the secret powers of nature. Ceremonial magic, on the other hand, especially the magic of the books called Grimoires, is within either a Jewish or Christian cabalistic framework.

An exception to this latter rule, however is the system used by the magical order known as the Golden Dawn. This association was founded by S. L. MacGregor Mathers, Dr. William Woodman, and Dr. Wynn Westcott, in 1887, from Rosicrucian sources. It has been the parent body of most serious magical orders of modern times.

Its system seeks to harmonise the old cabalistic magic with the invocation of the ancient gods. It owes much to the poetic vision of W. B. Yeats, who was a member of the Order. Incidentally, he too once resided at Steyning in Sussex.

𝔅𝔦𝔟𝔩𝔦𝔬𝔤𝔯𝔞𝔭𝔥𝔶

AHMED, Rollo	The Black Art. London, 1936
AITCHISON, George	Unknown Brighton. London, 1926
BARING-GOULD, Rev. S. A.	Book of Folk-Lore. London, N. D.
BECKETT, Arthur	The Spirit of the Downs. London, 1949
BRUCE-MITFORD, R. L. S. (Editor)	Recent Archaeological Excavations in Britain. London, 1956
CALDER-MARSHALL, Arthur	The Magic of My Youth. London, 1951
CROWLEY, Aleister	Magick in Theory and Practice. Privately printed, 1929
ELWORTHY, Frederick Thomas	The Evil Eye. London, 1895
ELWORTHY, Frederick Thomas	Horns of Honour. London, 1900
ERREDGE, J. A.	History of Brighthelmston. Brighton, 1862
EWEN, C. L'Estrange	Witch Hunting and Witch Trials. London, 1929
FABIAN, Ex-Supt. Robert	London After Dark. London, 1954
FLEET, C.	Glimpses of our Ancestors in Sussex (2nd Series). Lewes, 1882
GRAVES, Robert	The Greek Myths. London, 1957
HARRIS, Rendel	The Ascent of Olympus. Manchester, 1917
HOLE, Christina	English Folklore. London, 1940
HOLE, Christina	Witchcraft in England. London, 1945
HOLE, Christina	English Shrines and Sanctuaries. London, 1954
HOLE, Christina	A Mirror of Witchcraft. London, 1956
HONE, William	The Every-Day Book. London, 1826-7

HOPE, Robert Charles — The Legendary Lore of the Holy Wells of England. London, 1893

HOPKINS, R. Thurston — Ghosts Over England. London, 1953

HOPKINS, R. Thurston — The World's Strangest Ghost Stories. London, 1955

KNIGHT, Richard Payne (and WRIGHT, Thomas) — Two Essays on the Worship of Priapus. London, 1894

LATHAM, Charlotte — Some West Sussex Superstitions. 1868 (See The Folk-Lore Record, Vol. I.)

LAYARD, John — The Lady of the Hare. London, 1944

LEA, Henry Charles — Materials Towards a History of Witchcraft. Pennsylvania, 1939

LELAND, Charles Godfrey — Etruscan Roman Remains. London, 1892

LELAND, Charles Godfrey — Aradia: the Gospel of the Witches. London, 1899

LEVI, Eliphas — Transcendental Magic: its Doctrine and Ritual. London, 1896

MacCULLOCH, Rev. J. A. — The Celts and Scandinavian Religions. London, 1948

MACKAY, Charles — Memoirs of Extraordinary Popular Delusions. London, 1852

MURRAY, Margaret Alice — The Witch Cult in Western Europe. Oxford, 1921

MURRAY, Margaret Alice — The God of the Witches. London, 1952

PREVOST-BATTERSBY, H. F. — Man Outside Himself: the Facts of Etheric Projection. London, N. D.

SCOTT, Sir Walter — Letters on Demonology and Witchcraft. London, 1830

SPENCE, Lewis — The Minor Traditions of British Mythology. London, 1948

THOMAS, Dylan

THOMPSON, R. Lowe

UDALL, J. S.

Collected Poems. London, 1957

The History of the Devil: the Horned God of the West. London, 1929

Dorsetshire Folk-Lore. Hertford, 1922

FEATURES:

Folk-Lore

Historical MSS Commission

Illustrated

Transactions of the Folk-Lore Society

Vol. 13, Part 4. (Rye Papers)

September 27th 1952. Article, Witchcraft in Britain, by Allen Andrews

Journal of the English Folk Song Vol. 8, 1957
and Dance Society

Oxford English Dictionary   1933

Sussex Archaeological Collections

Sussex County Magazine

Sussex Notes and Queries

Sunday Empire News   November 1st 1959

Sunday Graphic   June 10th 1956

Sunday Pictorial   November 7th 1954

Sunday Pictorial   June 29th 1958

Sunday Pictorial   October 5th 1958

The Times   September 27th 1920

The Times   October 7th 9th and 14th 1931

The Times   March 2nd 1956

Herbert Samuel Toms (1874-1940)

Herbert Toms was a curator at Brighton Museum and Art Gallery from 1897 to 1939. He was a lively spirit fascinated by Sussex folklore, history and archaeology. He had realised his passion for archaeology before arriving in Brighton, whilst working in Dorset as an assistant to General Pitt-Rivers. Pitt-Rivers is widely regarded as the first scientific archaeologist to work in Britain. On moving to Brighton, Toms noticed that Sussex's local antiquities and traditions were rapidly disappearing, and so in 1906, he led several amateur archaeologists to found the Brighton & Hove Archaeological Club (later Society). Toms married Lady Pitt-Rivers' Breton maid, Christina. Together they shared a passion for folklore and archaeology and she soon started to lecture in these subjects. Christina died of cancer in 1927. Toms was devastated and around this time became a serious collector of Sussex folklore and a subscriber to Psychic News. He amassed an important archive of objects and rigorously recorded the history surrounding these personal artefacts, taking photographs of the items in situ and interviewing their owners at a time when country lore was in a state of rapid decline. He never accepted that technology and artefacts were more worthy subjects for study than human beliefs and customs. His archive remains with Brighton & Hove's museum service and it seems more than likely that Doreen Valiente had access to Toms' work whilst researching for this book.

Index

☙ Dedication

Tony MacLeod, Woodsman, observer of life, family man, Cunning man and Witch.

Having spent most of my life working in fields and woodland, due in no small part to Doreen, the question of "Where Witchcraft Lives" is for me a simple one. In short it is love, and it is all around us, it is in the soil, the wind, the sun, the moon and the stars, it is in the stones and the trees of our land and therefore in our very blood and bones. The white, or witch-hare, is a common legend throughout many rural areas of our Isle; stories of which encapsulate the connection to the wild magick of our land, an inspiration in itself, of becoming one with all; an acceptance of our natural instincts.

Many years ago, Doreen showed me that in order to find the wild natural magick, one was to look beyond and often into the wild places of nature, so I did, I found it and learned to work with it on many levels, both practically and esoterically. I still look, I still find and I am still learning to work with it today. For my work and my name to appear on the same publication as Doreen Valiente is a complete pinnacle in my life and a true honour.

This lady's work set me upon the path many years ago, Thank you Doreen, and may you continue to watch over this wayward child - Flags, Flax and Fodder.

Doreen Valiente (1922 - 1999)

109

The Doreen Valiente Foundation

The Doreen Valiente Foundation is a charitable trust dedicated to the protection and preservation of material relating to Pagan practices, spirituality and religion. The Foundation is also dedicated to researching and interpreting this material and making such research and the material itself accessible to the public for the benefit of wider education and the advancement of knowledge in this unique landscape of living cultural and religious heritage.

The Foundation was established in 2011 and received legal ownership of Doreen Valiente's entire legacy of artefacts, books, writings, documents, manuscripts and copyrights under a deed of trust that permanently prevents the sale or splitting up of the collection and prohibits the making of profit through exploitation of the collection. This means that every penny earned by the Foundation, including the proceeds of the sale of this book) is spent on persuing its goals and charitable objects as above.

The Foundation runs a number of ongoing projects, working towards the establishment of a permanent museum home for the collection and the physical creation of a Centre For Pagan Studies which was the name of the organisation of which Doreen was patron shortly before her death in 1999. The Foundation succeeded in a campaign to have Doreen awarded a Heritage Blue Plaque which was unveiled at her former home in Brighton, England in 2013 and has ongoing plans to honour other important Pagan figures in a similar way - at the time of publication the campaign for Gerald Gardner's blue plaque is underway. The Foundation is also organising conferences, talks and exhibitions as well as engaging with the global community in matters of religious history and heritage.

More information about Doreen Valiente and The Doreen Valiente Foundation, including foundation membership, details of events and activities, purchase of Doreen Valiente merchandise, books etc and donations can be found at:

www.doreenvaliente.org

Printed in the USA
CPSIA information can be obtained
at www.ICGtesting.com
LVHW012331300723
753896LV00012B/673